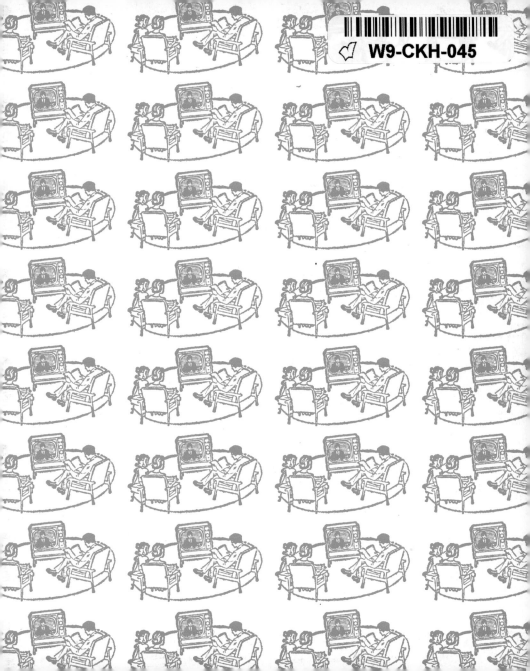

TV MANIA

A TIMELINE OF TELEVISION

TV MANIA

Edith Pavese & Judith Henry

HARRY N. ABRAMS, INC., PUBLISHERS

Library of Congress Cataloging-in-Publication Data

Pavese, Edith M.
TV mania : a timeline of television / Edith Pavese & Judith Henry.
p. cm.
ISBN 0-8109-3892-8
1. Television programs—United States—Chronology. I. Henry, Judith.
II. Title.
PN1992.3.U5P38 1998
791.45'75'0973—dc21   98-6423

Printed and bound in Italy

Harry N. Abrams, Inc.
100 Fifth Avenue
New York, N.Y. 10011
www.abramsbooks.com

INTRODUCTION

Considered a "magic window on the world" at its beginnings, television has been, over the years, controversial, even maligned as being dangerous—and also praised as a medium that brings us together (we remember The Beatles on *The Ed Sullivan Show*, "Who Shot J.R.?," the mini-series *Roots*, the last episodes of *M*A*S*H* and *Seinfeld*).

Television has been called the most important form of mass communication since Gutenberg's printing press, and, in fact, it affects almost everyone throughout the world (there are very few places where there are no television sets). People have been known to choose a television before indoor plumbing or heat or even a telephone.

Although the idea of mass communication was introduced with the radio, television gets its power from its images, the visual impact. The fact that the history of television has occurred within recent memory, a self-contained fifty years or so, makes it dynamic and accessible (although we lack perspective). In the pre-computer era, television was the hot medium, the one we all knew and didn't have to "master." We just turned on the tube and entertainment flowed to us in a never-ending stream.

In creating **TV MANIA**, this celebration of network television programming, we decided to focus on the entertainment side of television content, the programs and the stars, the moments we like to remember. The enjoyment of this book comes from flipping through the pages, stopping anywhere—the equivalent of channel surfing. Our love affair with television has kept us tuning in over and over again. We can't get enough of it.

In this volume, the images have been selected from network archives, from publicity files, and from historical sources. The timeline follows moments in TV history year by year from its beginning through the present season. Shows are listed by the date of their first airing. The network on which they premiered is also listed, as are the initial cast members (except where noted).

We have had fun putting this book together and we hope that you enjoy it as much. So sit back...remember...look for your favorite stars and shows...and in between browsing through this book...turn on the television and enjoy our ever-changing companion.

E.P. and J.H.
New York City, 1998

"It's Howdy Doody Time!" Bob Smith helped to create one of the most memorable puppets of all time, HOWDY DOODY (carved by a member of the Walt Disney studios). Smith played Buffalo Bob (because he was from Buffalo, New York) and was the voice of Howdy Doody. He was joined by Clarabell the clown (played by Bob Keeshan, who later became Captain Kangaroo), who never spoke but had a number of noisemakers that made his intentions very clear to the Peanut Gallery (boys and girls who were guests on the show) and kids at home.

June 20, 1948: The premiere broadcast of the variety show TOAST OF THE TOWN hosted by Ed Sullivan. This first show featured Dean Martin and Jerry Lewis, Rodgers and Hammerstein, Eugene List, Jim Kirkwood, Ruby Goldstein, Lee Goodman, Monica Lewis, Kathryn Lee, and John Kokoman. In the front row are the original June Taylor Dancers.

1909 The word "television" is first used. **1927** Utah native Philo T. Farnsworth invents and files a patent for an all-electronic television image (about this same time, many other patents are also granted). *The Jazz Singer*, the first talking movie, is released. **1930** U.S. population 123 million; one in five Americans owns a car. **1931** RCA puts a TV antenna atop the Empire State Building. **1936** NBC unveils a television studio at Rockefeller Center, New York City; they produce a show that is reviewed by critics; Betty Goodwin, the first TV announcer, uses white face makeup and black lipstick. **1939** Television is introduced to the public at the World's Fair. **1946** U.S. population c.150 million. Beginning of regular network television. **1947 May 7 KRAFT TELEVISON THEATRE** (NBC) debuts. It is the first regularly scheduled drama program. The **WORLD SERIES** between the victorious New York Yankees and the Brooklyn Dodgers is broadcast. **1948** Fewer than 2 percent of U.S. homes have a TV set. **June 8 THE MILTON BERLE SHOW (TEXACO STAR THEATER)** (NBC). "Oh we're the men of Texaco, we work from Maine to Mexico." Basically a vaudeville format beginning and ending with Berle who also appeared throughout the show in various skits.

MILTON BERLE brought his nightclub act to television and folks rushed home (or visited a neighbor lucky enough to own a TV set) to see him. In fact, movie theaters and restaurants were usually empty on Tuesday evenings when "Uncle Miltie" was on the small screen. Milton Berle became "Mr. Television."

June 20, **THE ED SULLIVAN SHOW (TOAST OF THE TOWN)** (CBS). The budget for the first variety show was $1375 (including $375 for "talent"). Among those who made their TV debuts on the show: Bob Hope, Lena Horne, Eddie Fisher, Dinah Shore. **August 10 CANDID CAMERA** (CBS). Allen Funt's "Smile, you're on Candid Camera" was the explanatory phrase that greeted ordinary people put in awkward, but usually good-natured, funny situations filmed by the Candid Camera team. **November 2** All networks run **PRESIDENTIAL ELECTION COVERAGE** (Harry S. Truman was the winner). Results

"Yoo, hoo Mrs. Goldberg" brought Molly Goldberg (Gertrude Berg, who also wrote and produced the show) to her window. Molly helped her neighbors and gossiped with them. THE GOLDBERGS—mother, father, son, and daughter—lived at 1030 East Tremont Avenue in the Bronx, New York.

1949: One of the first Western series on TV was HOPALONG CASSIDY. "Hoppy" (William Boyd) is seen here with Robert Mitchum in a show entitled "Hoppy Serves a Writ." Hoppy was a gentler cowboy than usually seen, but he always got the villain anyway.

The very active game show BEAT THE CLOCK began in 1950 with Bud Collyer as emcee. Contestants chosen from the audience had to complete hilarious stunts (which often involved pies, whipped cream, and water) before the big studio clock ticked down the suspenseful minutes.

are broadcast worldwide. **November 29 KUKLA, FRAN AND OLLIE** (NBC). Fran Allison hosted and was a star with puppeteer Burr Tillstrom's Kukla (very serious), Ollie (a friendly dragon), and others. **December 6 ARTHUR GODFREY'S TALENT SCOUTS** (CBS). Godfrey hosted a show for amateur (and some professional) talent. **1949 January 10 THE GOLDBERGS** (starring Gertrude Berg) (CBS). This highly successful warm family comedy had run for 20 years on radio. Molly and husband Jake (Philip Loeb), son Sammy (Larry Robinson), daughter Rosalie (Arlene McQuade),

along with Uncle David (Eli Mintz) were a Jewish family living in the Bronx. **January 12 ARTHUR GODFREY AND HIS FRIENDS** (CBS). A variety show. **January 20 INAUGURATION OF HARRY S. TRUMAN** on all networks. **June 24 HOPALONG CASSIDY** (NBC). "Hoppy" (William Boyd) and his horse Topper moved from movie versions of this cowboy's adventures to TV. Boyd owned the rights to his films and parlayed that into a highly successful TV series.

June 27 CAPTAIN VIDEO AND HIS VIDEO RANGERS (DuMont). Captain Video (Richard Coogan, who was playing opposite John Garfield on Broadway at the same time), The Ranger (Don Hastings), Dr. Pauli (Hal Conklin). "Guardian of the Safety of the World," Captain Video was a citizen who worked from "a private mountain hideaway, sometime in the 21st or 22nd century." He invented futuristic weapons to battle his nemeses, Nargola, Mook the Moon Man, Dr. Clysmok. The initial prop budget was $25 per show and many items were made from off-the-shelf automobile parts. One of the first shows anywhere to have tie-in product licensing—it offered decoder rings, space helmets, and various weapons to viewers. Names for the weapons were: Discatron, Radio Scillograph, Cosmic Ray Vibrator that countered the evil Trisonic Compensator (owned by evil Dr. Pauli). **1950**

February 16 WHAT'S MY LINE (CBS), ran for 17 years. Moderator John Daly; Panelists Arlene Francis, Dorothy Kilgallen, Louis Untermeyer, Hal Block, Bennett Cerf, Steve Allen (who created the "Is it bigger than a breadbox?" query), Fred Allen. **February 25 YOUR SHOW OF SHOWS** (NBC). This 90-minute live show centered on the comic brilliance of Sid Caesar and Imogene Coca, who spoofed everything from pretentious inter-

Classic comedy from **YOUR SHOW OF SHOWS** starring Sid Caesar, Imogene Coca, and regulars Howard Morris and Carl Reiner. The show was a live 90-minute comedy. The brilliant team of writers included Mel Brooks, Woody Allen, Larry Gelbart, Neil Simon, Mel Tolkin, and Lucille Kallen. Caesar's innate ability to mimic any dialect or language provided some of the funniest moments. Here Caesar plays the Professor to Coca's ballerina.

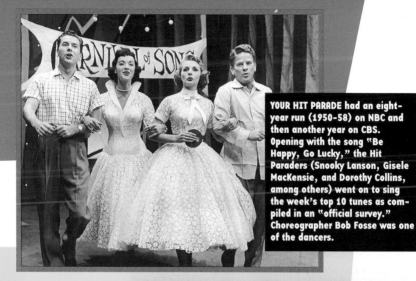

YOUR HIT PARADE had an eight-year run (1950-58) on NBC and then another year on CBS. Opening with the song "Be Happy, Go Lucky," the Hit Paraders (Snooky Lanson, Gisele MacKensie, and Dorothy Collins, among others) went on to sing the week's top 10 tunes as compiled in an "official survey." Choreographer Bob Fosse was one of the dancers.

views to famous movies and created a series of memorable characters. **March 23 BEAT THE CLOCK** (CBS). Contestants had to complete stunts within a time limit. Prizes (low monetary value) and a "bonus prize" were given for successful completion. **July 10 YOUR HIT PARADE** (NBC). Eileen Wilson, Snooky Lanson, Dorothy Collins, singers. The Hit Paraders dancers and chorus performed the nation's top 10 songs for that week as compiled by an "official survey"; Andre Baruch, announcer. **September 3 MISS TELEVISION USA PAGEANT** (DuMont), won by Edie Adams.

MAMA: A long-running gentle comedy that began in 1949. "I remember my brother Nels, and my little sister Dagmar, and, of course, Papa, but most of all...I remember Mama." Mama Marta Hansen was played by Peggy Wood; other cast members included Judson Laire as Papa Lars, Iris Mann (replaced by Robin Morgan), Rosemary Rice, and a young Dick Van Patten, who as an adult starred in *Eight is Enough*. The Hansens lived on Steiner Street in San Francisco.

Brilliant improvisationalist and comedian Ernie Kovacs embraced the television medium using a number of innovative camera and lighting techniques. Kovacs was on air from 1951 in a number of different shows. He is seen here as host of his "guess the identity of the guest" game show TAKE A GOOD LOOK, which ran from 1959-61.

October 5 YOU BET YOUR LIFE (NBC). Groucho Marx, host; George Fenneman, announcer (and straight man for Marx). Contestants had to answer simple questions for the prize money, but they also had to face the humorous barbs by master comedian Groucho (one of the famous Marx Brothers). If they mentioned the day's "secret word," which the audience knew ("It's a common word, something you see everyday"), a stuffed duck would drop down from the ceiling with $100 extra bonus in its mouth. The joy of the show was Marx's ability to ad lib clever repartee. If contestants lost all they could recoup by answering a question ("Who is buried in Grant's Tomb?") for a "consolation prize." **October 28 THE JACK BENNY SHOW** (CBS). Jack Benny had been a star on radio since 1932. Forever "39," stingy, and a halting violin player, the character of Benny on the show was the opposite of the generous, talented real-life Benny, a master of comic timing who could get a laugh just by waiting a second or two before responding. **December 25 THE STEVE ALLEN SHOW** (CBS). The earliest version of the night-time talk show. Allen had a few guests each evening (five nights a week) with whom he conducted off-the-cuff hilarious interviews. Allen

919

920

I LOVE LUCY. Still shown in reruns around the globe. Thought to be one of the greatest comedy classics, this is the one against which all others are measured. This instant hit starred the brilliantly talented Lucille Ball and Desi Arnaz (at center) and Vivian Vance (as Ethel Mertz) and William Frawley (as Fred Mertz).

September 11 SPACE PATROL (ABC). Commander of the Space Patrol Buzz Corey (Ed Kemmer) defended the United Planets of the Universe, Cadet Happy (Lyn Osborn) was his young assistant, bad-girl-turned-good Tonga (Nina Bara), Maj. Robbie Robertson (Ken Mayer), Secy. Gen. of the United Planets (Norman Jolley), his daughter Carol Karlyle (Virginia Hewitt). The miracle of time travel allowed the protagonists to leave the 30th century A.D. for various adventures. **July 2** Ernie Kovacs, the brilliant comedian and improviser, hosted **ERNIE IN KOVACSLAND** (NBC), a live half-hour

KUKLA, FRAN, AND OLLIE. Puppets Kukla and Ollie (created by Burr Tillstrom, who also provided their voices) were beloved friends of children and adults from 1948 to 1957. Here they face Fran Allison, the puppets' human sidekick. Fran stood in front of the raised stage on which the puppets were placed. The show was done without precise scripts and relied on the ad lib skills of Tillstrom and Allison.

1951

show that highlighted the comic's visual genius. **July 4 STRIKE IT RICH.** (CBS). Emcee Warren Hull. Contestants on this quiz show were in need of financial help. **September 4 FIRST COAST-TO-COAST TELECAST** showed President Truman's speech in San Francisco at the Japanese Peace Treaty Conference (all networks). **October 15 I LOVE LUCY** (CBS) was an instant comedy hit. Starring Lucille Ball (as wacky Lucy), Desi Arnaz (as her husband Ricky Ricardo, Cuban bandleader at the Tropicana nightclub), Vivian Vance (neighbor and friend Ethel Mertz), William Frawley (neighbor, landlord, and friend Fred Mertz) as the ensemble cast that got into glorious scrapes each week.

Beginning in 1951 (first as a daytime program, then in the evening as well), STRIKE IT RICH tugged on America's heartstrings. Audience members in need of help (usually financial), after telling their sad stories, could participate in a simple quiz that almost guaranteed that they would be winners. The show also opened up its call-in "Heart Line" which brought in additional donations from viewers.

November 18 SEE IT NOW (CBS). Commentator Edward R. Murrow goes on air with the first news documentary (produced by Fred Friendly), also the first live, coast-to-coast commercial broadcast, using a split screen to show simultaneously the Brooklyn and the Golden Gate bridges. **December 23** First network coverage of an **NFL CHAMPIONSHIP GAME** (DuMont). **December 24 AMAHL AND THE NIGHT VISITORS** (NBC). Christmas opera by GianCarlo Menotti. **1952 January 3 DRAGNET** (NBC). Theme music "dum-de-dum-dum." Unusual for its time with realistic, deliberately gritty, slow-paced dialogue: "The story you are about to hear is true, only the names have been changed to protect the innocent." At the end of the program, the announcer would give details of the criminal's conviction and sentence. **May 3 FIRST LIVE COVERAGE OF A HORSE RACE,** the Kentucky Derby (CBS). **June 19 I'VE GOT A SECRET** (CBS). The show is remembered for moderator Gary Moore, with Bill Cullen, Henry Morgan, Faye Emerson, and Jayne Meadows as panelists who questioned the contestant, including a celebrity, to guess the secret shown on screen to home viewers. The contestant

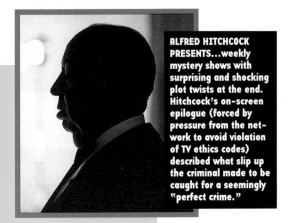

ALFRED HITCHCOCK PRESENTS...weekly mystery shows with surprising and shocking plot twists at the end. Hitchcock's on-screen epilogue (forced by pressure from the network to avoid violation of TV ethics codes) described what slip up the criminal made to be caught for a seemingly "perfect crime."

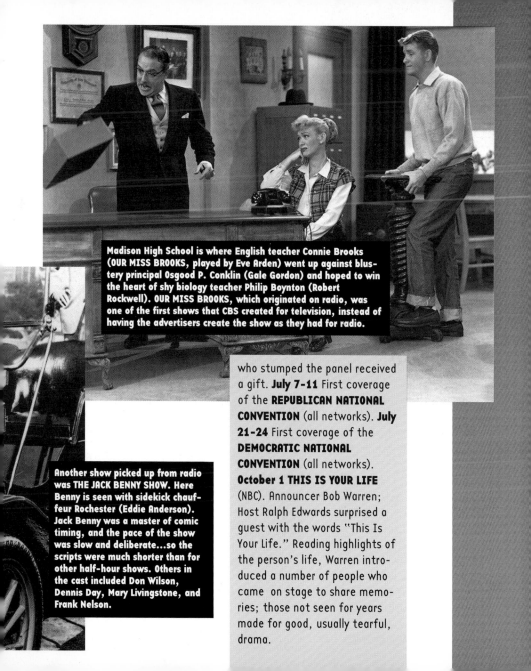

Madison High School is where English teacher Connie Brooks (OUR MISS BROOKS, played by Eve Arden) went up against blustery principal Osgood P. Conklin (Gale Gordon) and hoped to win the heart of shy biology teacher Philip Boynton (Robert Rockwell). OUR MISS BROOKS, which originated on radio, was one of the first shows that CBS created for television, instead of having the advertisers create the show as they had for radio.

Another show picked up from radio was THE JACK BENNY SHOW. Here Benny is seen with sidekick chauffeur Rochester (Eddie Anderson). Jack Benny was a master of comic timing, and the pace of the show was slow and deliberate...so the scripts were much shorter than for other half-hour shows. Others in the cast included Don Wilson, Dennis Day, Mary Livingstone, and Frank Nelson.

who stumped the panel received a gift. **July 7-11** First coverage of the **REPUBLICAN NATIONAL CONVENTION** (all networks). **July 21-24** First coverage of the **DEMOCRATIC NATIONAL CONVENTION** (all networks). **October 1 THIS IS YOUR LIFE** (NBC). Announcer Bob Warren; Host Ralph Edwards surprised a guest with the words "This Is Your Life." Reading highlights of the person's life, Warren introduced a number of people who came on stage to share memories; those not seen for years made for good, usually tearful, drama.

October 3 OUR MISS BROOKS
(CBS). Originated on radio in
1948, it starred Eve Arden
(Connie Brooks, English teacher
at Madison High School) and Gale
Gordon (Osgood P. Conklin,
Principal, always berating Miss
Brooks), Robert Rockwell (Philip
Boynton, eligible biology
teacher), Richard Crenna (Walter
Denton, slow student). **October 3**
THE ADVENTURES OF OZZIE &
HARRIET (ABC). Long-running
family show (1952-66): Ozzie,
Harriet, David, and Eric "Ricky."
October 14 THE RED BUTTONS

OZZIE & HARRIET. The quintessential 1950s couple with their
real-life sons. The Nelson family
(Ozzie, Harriet, David and Ricky)
lived in the public eye. Ricky, who
played a rock 'n roll star on the
show, became a teen idol who
sold millions of records.

SHOW (CBS). "Ho, ho...He, he...Ha, ha" the opening song became a national craze. Buttons was a skilled comic vaudevillian. **December 30 THE ERNIE KOVACS SHOW** (CBS/NBC 1956). Ernie Kovacs, Edie Adams. Wacky offbeat humor was created by Ernie (with ever-present cigar) with a series of comedy sketches. Among the favorite characters were The Nairobi Trio, poet Percy Dovetonsils, and The Question Man.

In 1952, THE RED BUTTONS SHOW, a comedy/variety program, was at the top and Buttons himself was on the cover of *Time* magazine.

ARTHUR GODFREY'S TALENT SCOUTS. The first of four Arthur Godfrey series to air. Perhaps Godfrey's greatest talent was his ability to discover talent in others. Pat Boone and The McGuire Sisters were among those featured on this show.

Beginning in 1952, host Ralph Edwards surprised a guest by announcing "THIS IS YOUR LIFE!" and by bringing old friends and family members not seen for years on stage. Tears and laughter were the emotions that riveted audience members. Guests were usually not celebrities, but here, on an October 29, 1952 airing, we see Casey Stengel.

1953 March 19 First coast-to-coast **TELEVISED "OSCARS"** (Academy of Motion Picture Arts and Sciences Awards) coverage (NBC). Bob Hope, host. The ceremony ran too long and was cut off before it ended. **June 2 CORONATION OF QUEEN ELIZABETH II** (CBS/NBC). Filmed. **November 22 LIFE WITH FATHER** (CBS). Father Clarence Day, Sr. (Leon Ames), wife Vinnie Day (Lurene Tuttle), Clarence Day, Jr. (Ralph Reed), Whitney Day (Ronald Keith). Based on essays by Clarence Day, Jr., that

"My name is Friday...I'm a cop." Known for its laconic dialogue ("Just the facts, ma'am"), DRAGNET was one of the earliest cop shows. Each week Sgt. Joe Friday (played by Jack Webb, who also directed) and his partner solved a crime based on a true case.

LIFE WITH FATHER, set in the 1890s in New York, starred Leon Ames, Lurene Tuttle, Ralph Reed, and Ronald Keith as members of the Day family. The show was based on a series of essays, a book, and a play—all more successful than this TV show.

appeared in *The New Yorker*. **1954 April 22 to June 17** The **ARMY-MCCARTHY HEARINGS** (live on ABC/DuMont). Sen. Joseph McCarthy's attempt to uncover communists in the army and the government. **September 11** First coast-to-coast televised **MISS AMERICA BEAUTY PAGEANT** (ABC). **September 12 LASSIE** (CBS). Jeff Miller (Tommy Rettig) lived on a farm with heroic companion Lassie. The series derived from *Lassie Come Home*, a 1940 book by Eric Knight; then a 1943 film with Roddy McDowall and Elizabeth Taylor. **September 13 MEDIC** (NBC). Set in L.A. and starring Richard Boone as Dr. Konrad Styner, it was the first medical drama to be filmed in real hospitals and the first to show the birth of a baby. **September 27 THE TONIGHT SHOW (TONIGHT)** (NBC). Steve Allen, host; Gene Rayburn, announcer; Skitch Henderson and His Orchestra. Allen opened the live show at his piano and then would move to a desk where he chatted and interviewed guests. Among others who appeared regularly were Steve Lawrence and Eydie Gorme, Andy Williams, Pat Marshall. Allen also interviewed audience members and created various comic skits. (In 1956 Ernie Kovacs became host.)

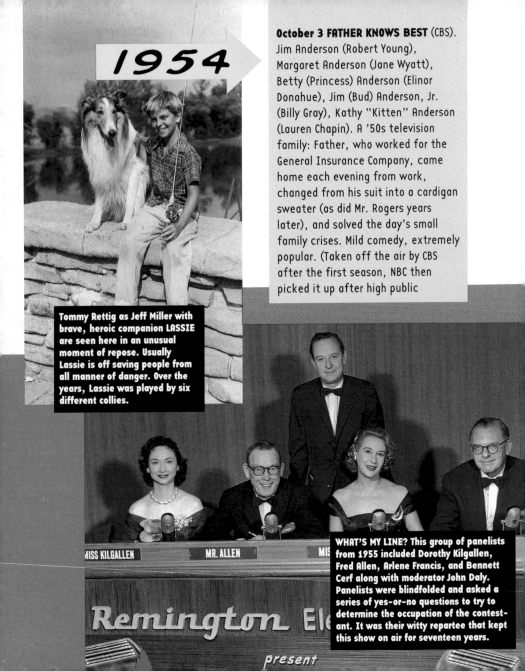

1954

October 3 FATHER KNOWS BEST (CBS). Jim Anderson (Robert Young), Margaret Anderson (Jane Wyatt), Betty (Princess) Anderson (Elinor Donahue), Jim (Bud) Anderson, Jr. (Billy Gray), Kathy "Kitten" Anderson (Lauren Chapin). A '50s television family: Father, who worked for the General Insurance Company, came home each evening from work, changed from his suit into a cardigan sweater (as did Mr. Rogers years later), and solved the day's small family crises. Mild comedy, extremely popular. (Taken off the air by CBS after the first season, NBC then picked it up after high public

Tommy Rettig as Jeff Miller with brave, heroic companion LASSIE are seen here in an unusual moment of repose. Usually Lassie is off saving people from all manner of danger. Over the years, Lassie was played by six different collies.

MISS KILGALLEN   MR. ALLEN   MIS

WHAT'S MY LINE? This group of panelists from 1955 included Dorothy Kilgallen, Fred Allen, Arlene Francis, and Bennett Cerf along with moderator John Daly. Panelists were blindfolded and asked a series of yes-or-no questions to try to determine the occupation of the contestant. It was their witty repartee that kept this show on air for seventeen years.

Remington Ele

present

FATHER KNOWS BEST. One of the quintessential 1950s families as we liked to imagine ourselves. In the small-town Anderson family headed by Jim (Robert Young) and Margaret (Jane Wyatt), there were few signs of strife and children grew up with minimal problems and no social rebellion.

demand.) **1955 March 7** First coast-to-coast televised **EMMY AWARDS** (NBC), hosted by Steve Allen. **June 7 THE $64,000 QUESTION** (CBS). Contestants could win large sums of money by answering questions in their fields of expertise. So they could concentrate, contestants entered soundproof "isolation booths." This was the first of the big-money quiz shows and in its first season replaced *I Love Lucy* as the number 1 show. Successful contestants could go on to the *$64,000 Challenge* and increase their winnings. *Question,* along with many other quiz shows, went off the air in 1958, amidst the scandal of quiz show "rigging." **July 2 THE**

LAWRENCE WELK SHOW (ABC). Lawrence Welk, host; George Cates, musical director. Welk's very traditional "Champagne Music" show was panned during its first season, but it stayed on the air for 16 successful years. Alice Lon, the "Champagne Lady," was fired for showing "too much knee" and thousands wrote in to protest. **September 6 THE LIFE AND LEGEND OF WYATT EARP** (ABC). Based on the real-life Marshal Wyatt Earp (played by Hugh O'Brien). The well-armed Earp, along with deputy Bat Masterson (Mason Alan Dinehart III) kept the peace in the Old West.

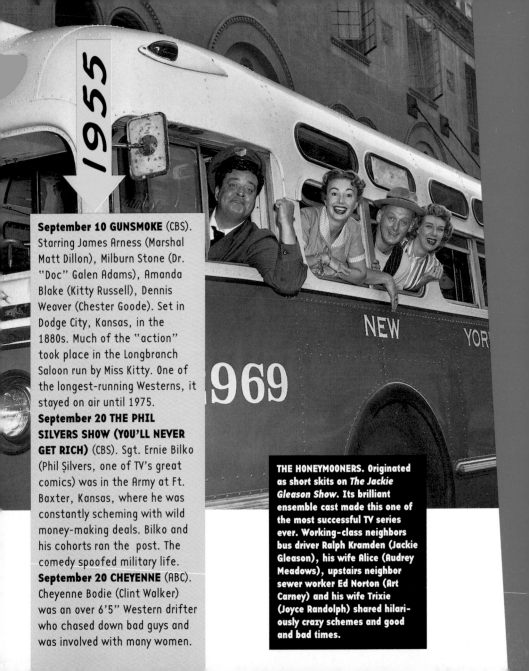

1955

September 10 GUNSMOKE (CBS). Starring James Arness (Marshal Matt Dillon), Milburn Stone (Dr. "Doc" Galen Adams), Amanda Blake (Kitty Russell), Dennis Weaver (Chester Goode). Set in Dodge City, Kansas, in the 1880s. Much of the "action" took place in the Longbranch Saloon run by Miss Kitty. One of the longest-running Westerns, it stayed on air until 1975.

September 20 THE PHIL SILVERS SHOW (YOU'LL NEVER GET RICH) (CBS). Sgt. Ernie Bilko (Phil Silvers, one of TV's great comics) was in the Army at Ft. Baxter, Kansas, where he was constantly scheming with wild money-making deals. Bilko and his cohorts ran the post. The comedy spoofed military life.

September 20 CHEYENNE (ABC). Cheyenne Bodie (Clint Walker) was an over 6'5" Western drifter who chased down bad guys and was involved with many women.

THE HONEYMOONERS. Originated as short skits on *The Jackie Gleason Show*. Its brilliant ensemble cast made this one of the most successful TV series ever. Working-class neighbors bus driver Ralph Kramden (Jackie Gleason), his wife Alice (Audrey Meadows), upstairs neighbor sewer worker Ed Norton (Art Carney) and his wife Trixie (Joyce Randolph) shared hilariously crazy schemes and good and bad times.

M-I-C-K-E-Y M-O-U-S-E. The song we all loved to sing along with child actors who were The Mouseketeers. THE MICKEY MOUSE CLUB had an adult host who led the Mouseketeers through the week's programs. Each day had a song and a special theme, such as "Circus Day" or "Anything Can Happen Day."

CAPTAIN KANGAROO (Bob Keeshan), here with guest Dudley Moore and puppet Mr. Moose, has been one of the mainstays of children's television programming. Gentle and warm, Captain Kangaroo appealed to youngsters for decades.

October 1 THE HONEYMOONERS (CBS). "One of these days, Alice...one of these days." Ralph Kramden (Jackie Gleason), Alice Kramden (Audrey Meadows), Ed Norton (Art Carney), Trixie Norton (Joyce Randolph). The concept for this show was first seen in 1951 on *The Cavalcade of Stars* (Pert Kelton played Alice). Comedy featuring working-class couples living in Brooklyn (unusual in the context of 1950s suburban ideals). Ralph (a bus driver) and his wife Alice and their upstairs neighbors Norton (who works in the sewers) and his wife Trixie. Ralph and Ed devise schemes to become rich or at least to

"Ah one, ah two..." Bandleader **LAWRENCE WELK** and his orchestra gave us the mellifluous sounds of "Champagne Music" for years. His show included some dance numbers, regular performers, and guest stars, but the attraction was the music.

advance their lot, which almost never come to fruition; the wives generally oppose the unrealistic ideas. Gleason's physical comedic timing and his perfectionism on the set set the tone. **October 2 ALFRED HITCHCOCK PRESENTS** (CBS). Alfred Hitchcock, seen in dark profile, introduced the show each week. These were tales of suspense, often with surprise endings in which the perpetrator of the crime seemed to "get away with murder." **1956 June 24 THE STEVE ALLEN SHOW** (NBC). Steve Allen was the host and star of this weekly comedy/variety show. Elvis Presley was a guest here before making his appearance on *The Ed Sullivan Show*. The Man on the Street Interview was one of the most remembered features of this show. **September 9 ELVIS PRESLEY** appears on *The Ed Sullivan Show* for the first time introducing rock 'n roll to millions. **September 12 TWENTY-ONE** (NBC). Jack Barry, host. Based on the card game twenty-one. Highly popular big-money quiz show. Ruined by the 1958 quiz show scandals of fixing.

THE MID-FIFTIES SAW THE INTRODUCTION OF THE "ADULT WESTERN." *THE LIFE AND LEGEND OF WYATT EARP* AND *GUNSMOKE* PREMIERED IN THE SAME WEEK, FOLLOWED TEN DAYS LATER BY *CHEYENNE*.

GUNSMOKE was set in Dodge City, Kansas, in the late 1800s. Main characters are Marshall Matt Dillon (James Arness), Chester Goode (Dennis Weaver), Longbranch Saloon keeper Kitty Russell (Amanda Blake). The part of Dillon was first offered to John Wayne, who declined.

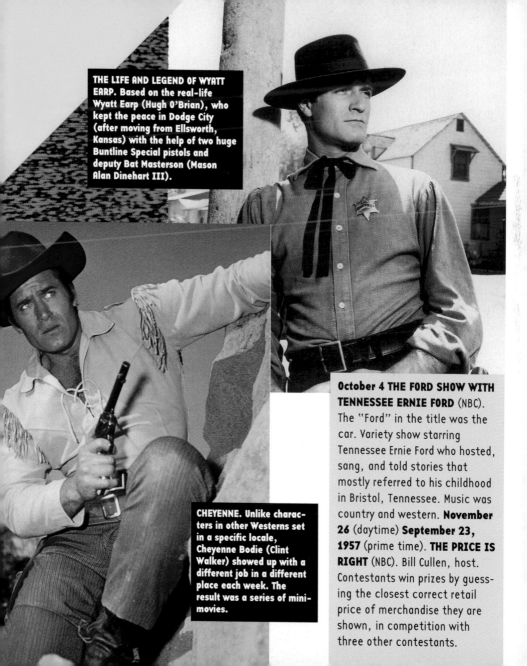

THE LIFE AND LEGEND OF WYATT EARP. Based on the real-life Wyatt Earp (Hugh O'Brian), who kept the peace in Dodge City (after moving from Ellsworth, Kansas) with the help of two huge Buntline Special pistols and deputy Bat Masterson (Mason Alan Dinehart III).

CHEYENNE. Unlike characters in other Westerns set in a specific locale, Cheyenne Bodie (Clint Walker) showed up with a different job in a different place each week. The result was a series of mini-movies.

October 4 THE FORD SHOW WITH TENNESSEE ERNIE FORD (NBC). The "Ford" in the title was the car. Variety show starring Tennessee Ernie Ford who hosted, sang, and told stories that mostly referred to his childhood in Bristol, Tennessee. Music was country and western. **November 26 (daytime) September 23, 1957 (prime time). THE PRICE IS RIGHT** (NBC). Bill Cullen, host. Contestants win prizes by guessing the closest correct retail price of merchandise they are shown, in competition with three other contestants.

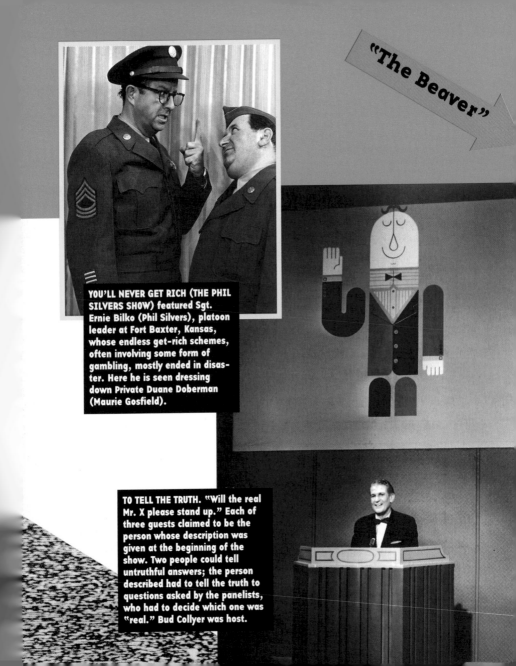

YOU'LL NEVER GET RICH (THE PHIL SILVERS SHOW) featured Sgt. Ernie Bilko (Phil Silvers), platoon leader at Fort Baxter, Kansas, whose endless get-rich schemes, often involving some form of gambling, mostly ended in disaster. Here he is seen dressing down Private Duane Doberman (Maurie Gosfield).

TO TELL THE TRUTH. "Will the real Mr. X please stand up." Each of three guests claimed to be the person whose description was given at the beginning of the show. Two people could tell untruthful answers; the person described had to tell the truth to questions asked by the panelists, who had to decide which one was "real." Bud Collyer was host.

LEAVE IT TO BEAVER. Here we have 1950s family values as portrayed with Jerry Mathers as cute seven-year-old "Beaver" Cleaver, whose best intentions often got him into trouble.

December 18 TO TELL THE TRUTH (CBS). Quiz show. Bud Collyer emcee; Kitty Carlisle, Polly Bergen, Hy Gardner, Hildy Parks, Ralph Bellamy (1957), panelists.
1957 January 19 THE ERNIE KOVACS SHOW (NBC), a wordless half-hour comedy special.
September 14 HAVE GUN, WILL TRAVEL (CBS). Main character Paladin (Richard Boone). This show became one of the most popular in the late '50s.
September 18 WAGON TRAIN (NBC). Wagon train master Maj. Seth Adams (Ward Bond), scout Flint McCullough (Robert Horton), head wagon driver Bill Hawks (Terry Wilson). The wagon train traveled from Missouri to the West Coast. Known for good character portrayals.

1957

HAVE GUN WILL TRAVEL. Elegant, black-clad Paladin (Richard Boone) had a striking calling card with a white chess knight that said "Have Gun, Will Travel. Wire Paladin, San Francisco." Gun-for-hire Paladin lived in the Hotel Carlton. Unlike most other Western heroes, he wore all black, had attended West Point and headed West after the Civil War. The theme song, "The Ballad of Paladin," was sung by Johnny Western.

September 21 PERRY MASON (CBS). Trial lawyer, defense attorney Perry Mason (Raymond Burr), secretary/assistant Della Street (Barbara Hale), P.I. Paul Drake (William Hopper), D.A. Hamilton Burger (William Talman), Lt. Arthur Tragg (Ray Collins). Based on Erle Stanley Gardner books. Weekly mystery stories concluding with a trial at which Mason elicited the truth from a reluctant witness at the very end of the hour. **September 22 MAVERICK** (ABC). Bret Maverick (James Garner), Bart Maverick (Jack Kelly), Samantha Crawford (Diane Brewster). A Western played as satire. It spoofed other shows and itself. **October 4 LEAVE IT TO BEAVER** (CBS). Beaver Cleaver (Jerry Mathers), Wally Cleaver (Tony Dow), Ward Cleaver (Hugh Beaumont), June Cleaver (Barbara Billingsly), Eddie Haskell (Ken Osmond). Middle-class 1950s "family values" comedy. **October 7 AMERICAN BANDSTAND** (ABC). Dick Clark hosted this long-running program which began as a dance show in Philadelphia. Guest performers who lip-synched (often sent by companies pushing new records) sang hit tunes, and teenagers danced to those and other recorded songs. **October 10 ZORRO** (ABC). Theme song

("Zorro—the fox so cunning and free, Zorro—make the sign of the Z!") became a hit. Caped and masked Zorro (Don Diego de la Vega) (Guy Williams), and his mute and seemingly deaf servant Bernardo (Gene Sheldon), went out to avenge wrongs, to help the oppressed, and to battle evil Capt. Monastario (Britt Lomond). Zorro's sword fights were legendary as was his slashing mark of the "Z" at the sites of his conquests. **1958 September 6 WANTED: DEAD OR ALIVE** (CBS). Josh Randall (Steve McQueen) was a bounty hunter who could bring in his quarry "dead or alive" during the late 1800s in the West. His weapon was a Winchester carbine.

THE PRICE IS RIGHT, TV's longest-running game show. In one of the contests, participants have to guess the value of the item shown without going over the actual retail price. The person coming closest to the value wins the item. Studio audience members participate loudly and emotionally helping players decide whether to continue the bid or to "freeze."

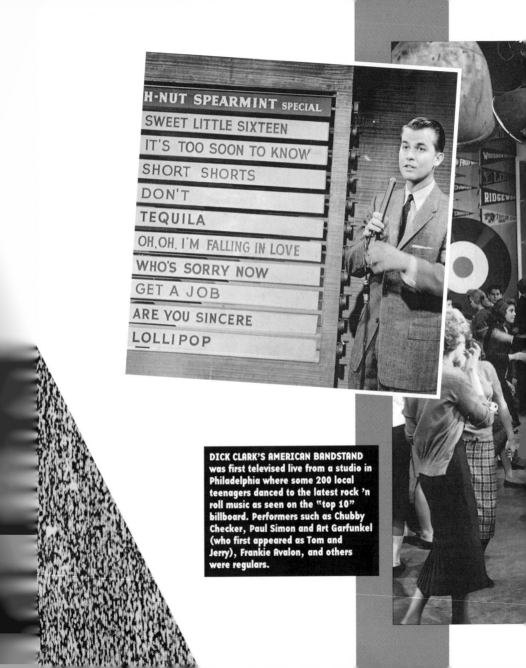

H-NUT SPEARMINT SPECIAL
SWEET LITTLE SIXTEEN
IT'S TOO SOON TO KNOW
SHORT SHORTS
DON'T
TEQUILA
OH, OH, I'M FALLING IN LOVE
WHO'S SORRY NOW
GET A JOB
ARE YOU SINCERE
LOLLIPOP

DICK CLARK'S AMERICAN BANDSTAND was first televised live from a studio in Philadelphia where some 200 local teenagers danced to the latest rock 'n roll music as seen on the "top 10" billboard. Performers such as Chubby Checker, Paul Simon and Art Garfunkel (who first appeared as Tom and Jerry), Frankie Avalon, and others were regulars.

1959 January 9 RAWHIDE (CBS). Gil Favor (Eric Fleming), Rowdy Yates (Clint Eastwood). "Rawhide" theme sung by Frankie Laine. Trail boss Favor and helper Yates moved cattle across the country.

September 12 BONANZA (NBC). First color TV Western. Ben Cartwright (Lorne Greene); sons Adam (Pernell Roberts), Little Joe (Michael Landon), Hoss (Dan Blocker); cook Hop Sing (Victor Sen Young). Patriarch Ben ran the Ponderosa Ranch (near Virginia City, Nevada) with his three sons.

September 29 DOBIE GILLIS (THE MANY LOVES OF DOBIE GILLIS) (CBS). Teenaged Dobie Gillis (Dwayne Hickman) was always on the lookout for beautiful girls, money, and special cars. Zelda (Sheila James) was trying to hook him. Good looking Milton (Warren Beatty) vied with Dobie for his girlfriend, Thalia (Tuesday Weld).

THE MANY LOVES OF DOBIE GILLIS. Dobie (Dwayne Hickman), a teenager crazy for girls, along with best friend Maynard G. Krebs (Bob Denver), and Zelda Gilroy (Sheila James), who was crazy for Dobie, tried to find the meaning of life in high school and beyond.

AS THE WORLD TURNS, set in the town of Oakdale, is one of the longest-running daytime soaps. It has the usual mix of deceit, love interests, death, illness, intrigue, money, success and failure, and always hard to unravel entanglements that endure for years.

DICK CLARK with singer Pat Boone in 1958.

THE MILLIONAIRE (1955) was everyone's dream. Each week billionaire John Beresford Tipton (never seen) had his secretary Michael Anthony (seen here at right) present a million-dollar cashier's check to an individual. The drama was provided by the reactions and plans of the recipients. The only "catch" for recipients was that they were told never to reveal where they received the money nor to search for the donor or they would forfeit the gift.

WAGON TRAIN master Major Seth Adams (Ward Bond, at right) and scout Flint McCullough (Robert Horton) left St. Joseph, Missouri, for the West Coast and faced a series of adventures, mishaps, and encounters with friendly and unfriendly folks along the way.

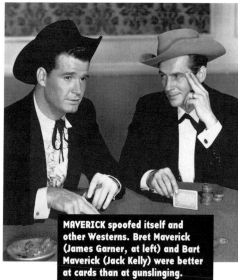

MAVERICK spoofed itself and other Westerns. Bret Maverick (James Garner, at left) and Bart Maverick (Jack Kelly) were better at cards than at gunslinging.

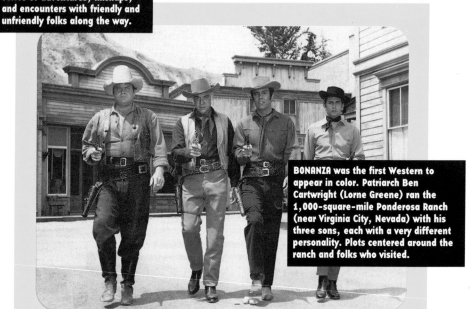

BONANZA was the first Western to appear in color. Patriarch Ben Cartwright (Lorne Greene) ran the 1,000-square-mile Ponderosa Ranch (near Virginia City, Nevada) with his three sons, each with a very different personality. Plots centered around the ranch and folks who visited.

ZORRO. Zorro's real identity is Don Diego de la Vega, a Spanish nobleman. Only Bernardo, a mute servant, and, later Don Alejandro, Don Diego's father, know Don Diego's secret identity. Mask-wearing Zorro is the "defender of the people" of California who combats an evil ruler. As with Superman's Clark Kent, Don Diego's temperament shown to the world is mild mannered and timid.

RAWHIDE (whose theme was sung by Frankie Laine) starred Clint Eastwood as Rowdy Yates who helped Gil Favor (Eric Fleming) move cattle across the country. His role here propelled Eastwood into stardom.

WANTED: DEAD OR ALIVE. Bounty hunter Josh Randall (Steve McQueen), with the help of a carbine he called "mare's leg," brought in his quarry "dead or alive." This show made McQueen a star (although he had just appeared in the film *The Blob*).

"Yabba dabba doo." THE FLINTSTONES, the first made-for-TV animated series, resembled a stone-age *Honeymooners*. Here Fred Flintstone (voice of Alan Reed) and his wife Wilma (Jean vander Pyl) share a loving moment. Their best friends are Barney Rubble (Mel Blanc) and Betty (Bea Benaderet and Gerry Johnson).

QUEEN FOR A DAY. Designed to bring tears to the eyes and prizes to the winner. Contestants chosen from the studio audience told tales of need and sorrow. Audience members would then select the most deserving of the five contestants, who would be crowned "Queen for a Day" and receive the prizes she most needed.

Hollywood-based private detectives Stu Bailey (Efrem Zimbalist, Jr.) and Jeff Spencer (Roger Smith) had their office at 77 SUNSET STRIP in Hollywood next to Dino's restaurant, where parking attendant Kookie (Edd Byrnes) worked and also wanted to help with cases. Kookie was known for constantly running a comb through his hair and for great lines such as "piling up the Zs" and "keep the eyeballs rolling."

October 2 THE TWILIGHT ZONE (CBS). Host Rod Serling introduced (and wrote 89 episodes) the eerie and well-wrought weekly dramas in this science fiction series. Almost every episode had a strange twist at the end. A cult classic. **October 15 THE UNTOUCHABLES** (ABC). Agent Eliot Ness (Robert Stack) led a group of agents (the "Untouchables") battling crime and corruption. **1960 September 26** Seventy million tune in to watch the first of the **KENNEDY-NIXON DEBATES** (all networks). Nixon's lack of TV charisma, which Kennedy had in abundance, may have cost him the election. People who only heard the debate thought Nixon had "won," but viewers saw the Kennedy magic.

Trial lawyer and defense attorney PERRY MASON (Raymond Burr) and P.I. Paul Drake (William Hopper) were a team that seemingly couldn't lose a case. In a predictable but still interesting format, Mason's skilled questioning of witnesses at the closing trial would always bring out the truth and solve the case.

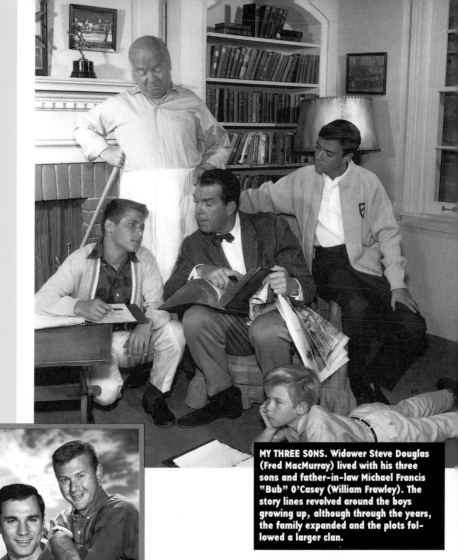

MY THREE SONS. Widower Steve Douglas (Fred MacMurray) lived with his three sons and father-in-law Michael Francis "Bub" O'Casey (William Frawley). The story lines revolved around the boys growing up, although through the years, the family expanded and the plots followed a larger clan.

The theme music for ROUTE 66 by Nelson Riddle was on the 1962 hit parade. The show featured Tod Stiles (Martin Milner), Buz Murdock (George Maharis) and a Corvette, in which they crossed the country in search of adventure and romance.

September 29 MY THREE SONS (ABC). Widower Steve Douglas (Fred MacMurray) lived with his three sons, Mike (Tim Considine), Robbie (Don Grady), and Chip (Stanley Livingston) and father-in-law "Bub" O'Casey (William Frawley, who played Fred Mertz on *I Love Lucy*). The show followed the boys and Steve's love interests.
September 30 THE FLINTSTONES (ABC). Characters are: Fred Flintstone works at Rock Head & Quarry Cave Construction Company; wife Wilma plays a Stoneway piano; daughter Pebbles; pet dinosaur Dino. Friends Barney and Betty Rubble adopt Bamm Bamm. Adults liked the show for its satire of suburban life. **1961 January 25** First live coverage of a **PRESIDENTIAL PRESS CONFERENCE** with President Kennedy (all networks). **September 28 DR. KILDARE** (NBC). Based on a series of films of the 1940s, the medical drama of life in Blair General Hospital featured young intern Dr. James Kildare and his mentor Dr. Leonard Gillespie.

One of the most violent shows when it came on air in 1959, THE UNTOUCHABLES fed our love of gangster lore. Eliot Ness (Robert Stack) led his group of Treasury agents (called "The Untouchables" by a Chicago newspaper) in a battle against crime. The real Ness was known as the man who pursued and brought Al Capone to justice.

DR. KILDARE. With wonderful episode titles such as "The Bell in the Schoolhouse Tolls for Thee, Kildare," the popular 1960s medical drama gave us a look at life in Blair General Hospital. Pictured are Dr. James Kildare (Richard Chamberlain), Dr. Leonard Gillespie (Raymond Massey), and Head Nurse Zoe Lawton (Lee Kurty).

I'VE GOT A SECRET. Guests (including a celebrity guest each week) shared their secret with host Garry Moore (at the same time that the viewers at home saw it flashed on their screens). Panelists then had to guess the secret. Winners received only an $80 prize, so the cleverness of the questions is what kept audiences coming back.

THE DICK VAN DYKE SHOW was conceived by master comedian Carl Reiner (who also played the part of Alan Brady). Rob Petrie (Dick Van Dyke), head writer for TV comedy, "The Alan Brady Show," was married to Laura Petrie (Mary Tyler Moore), a former dancer.

September 28 HAZEL (NBC). In this comedy, Hazel Burke (Shirley Booth) was the maid in the Baxter household, which she ran with an iron fist. Corporate lawyer George Baxter (Don DeFore) and wife Dorothy Baxter (Whitney Blake) were the couple of the house, who lived there with son Harold (Bobby Buntrock). **October 2 BEN CASEY** (ABC). Dr. Ben Casey (Vince Edwards), Dr. David Zorba (Sam Jaffe), Dr. Maggie Graham (Bettye Ackerman). Most popular of the early medical dramas (top show on ABC 1961/62 season) was set at County General Hospital. **October 3 THE DICK VAN DYKE SHOW** (CBS). This show was unpopular in its first season, but then became a solid hit. Rob Petrie (Dick Van Dyke), Laura Petrie (Mary Tyler Moore), Alan Brady (Carl Reiner). The show also used the talents of Morey Amsterdam who played Buddy Sorrell. **1962 February 20 SPACE FLIGHT** of Astronaut John Glenn orbiting the Earth (all networks).

Who worked for whom here? HAZEL (Shirley Booth), a housekeeper, who in her own way actually ran the Baxter household, which included corporate lawyer George Baxter ("Mr. B."), wife Dorothy, and son Harold. Hazel was based on a cartoon character created by Ted Key for the *Saturday Evening Post*.

September 23 THE JETSONS (ABC). A futuristic space-age cartoon family. Skypad Apartments was their home. Father George Jetson worked in the Spacely Space Age Sprockets plant. Mother Jane and children Judy and Elroy and dog Astro. Space "conveniences" abounded: the hydraulic lift that kept the apartment free of bad weather, the pneumatic tube used to send Elroy to school, the robot maid, and the atomic-powered bubble "car" for George. Additional characters' voices were provided by, among others, Mel Blanc, Hershel Bernardi, Howard Morris.

September 26 THE BEVERLY HILLBILLIES (CBS). The Clampett family moved to Beverly Hills from the Ozarks after oil found on their property made them millionaires. Theme song, "The Ballad of Jed Clampett," was on the 1964 hit parade. **1963**

September 17 THE FUGITIVE (ABC). Wrongfully sentenced to death for his wife's murder, Dr. Richard Kimble escaped when the prison train taking him to his execution derailed. His police escort, Lt. Philip Gerard, made it his mission to find him.

"There is a fifth dimension beyond that which is known to man. It is a dimension as vast as space and as timeless as infinity. It is the middle ground between light and shadow, between science and superstition, and it lies between the pit of man's fears and the summit of his knowledge. This is the dimension of the imagination. It is an area we call THE TWILIGHT ZONE." Here is William Shatner in "Nightmare at 20,000 Feet," one of the weekly tales.

THE GUIDING LIGHT, the longest-running daytime soap, began on radio in 1937 and on TV in 1952. It is still on the air. Here are actors Ellen Demming and Theo Goetz in a 1961 episode.

Their first widely-viewed live appearance was on THE ED SULLIVAN SHOW on February 9, 1964. As the audience went wild, they sang "I Want to Hold Your Hand," "All My Loving," "She Loves You," and "Till There Was You," among other instant hits.

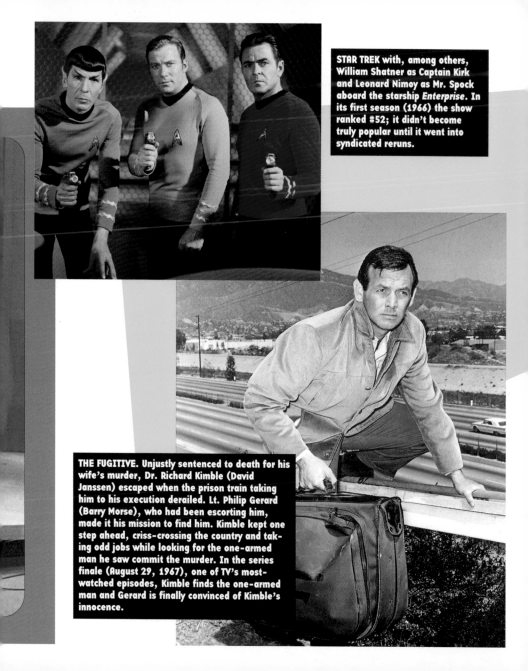

STAR TREK with, among others, William Shatner as Captain Kirk and Leonard Nimoy as Mr. Spock aboard the starship *Enterprise*. In its first season (1966) the show ranked #52; it didn't become truly popular until it went into syndicated reruns.

THE FUGITIVE. Unjustly sentenced to death for his wife's murder, Dr. Richard Kimble (David Janssen) escaped when the prison train taking him to his execution derailed. Lt. Philip Gerard (Barry Morse), who had been escorting him, made it his mission to find him. Kimble kept one step ahead, criss-crossing the country and taking odd jobs while looking for the one-armed man he saw commit the murder. In the series finale (August 29, 1967), one of TV's most-watched episodes, Kimble finds the one-armed man and Gerard is finally convinced of Kimble's innocence.

In 1961, its premiere year, BEN CASEY (Vince Edwards) was the top show for ABC and one of the most popular of the medical dramas. This one took place at County General Hospital and, with its powerful film sequences, captured the pace and drama of a large hospital. It can be considered the forerunner of today's *ER* and *Chicago Hope*.

AS THE WORLD TURNS, a daytime soap on air since 1956 (*The Edge of Night* premiered on the same day). Here in a February 1962 episode, we see cast members Don MacLaughlin, Eileen Fulton, and Helen Wagner.

Johnny Carson as The Great Carnac (Carnac the Magnificent) during his first season as host of THE TONIGHT SHOW in 1962. Carson reluctantly took over the program from host Jack Paar, but ended up staying with the show for 30 years. His comic timing and ability to ad lib with a range of guests made him one of the most popular late night hosts ever.

1963

September 24 PETTICOAT JUNCTION (CBS). The small town of Hooterville provided the setting for Kate Bradley's (Bea Benaderet) Shady Rest Hotel. Her three daughters: Billie Jo (Jeannine Riley), Bobbie Jo (Pat Woodell), and Betty Jo (Linda Kaye) had romances that formed the central motivation for the plots. **November 22-25 ASSASSINATION OF PRESIDENT JOHN KENNEDY** and following events leading to the funeral (all networks). **December 30** (daytime) **May 21, 1967** (prime time) **LET'S MAKE A DEAL** (NBC). Monty Hall, host; Jay Stewart, announcer. Studio audience members, usually dressed in silly costumes, traded items they had brought for hidden prizes, which ranged from worthless to highly valuable items.

THE JETSONS (on air in 1962) were a space-age family living in the Skypad Apartments in Orbit City. Father George worked in the Spacely Space Age Sprockets plant. The rest of the family were mother Jane, children Judy and Elroy, and the family dog Astro. Despite conveniences such as pneumatic tube travel and atomic-powered cars, the family situations were familiar to present-day viewers.

GILLIGAN'S ISLAND. An unlikely mix of hapless voyagers were marooned on a tropical island after their small ship, *The Minnow,* capsized in a storm. They tried for years to get off the island. Gilligan (one of the two crew members) was the most ambitious—and the most inept—in ever-failing plans for rescue.

April 10, 1964. Host Ernie Ford (at right) of THE TENNESSEE ERNIE FORD SHOW with guest Jack Benny.

1964 September 15 PEYTON PLACE (ABC). Based on the Grace Metalious novel, the series had all of the intrigue, sex, convoluted plot twists and surprises that had made the book a best seller. Constance MacKenzie Carson (Dorothy Malone) was a bookstore owner, her daughter Allison MacKenzie (Mia Farrow), Rodney Harrington (Ryan O'Neal) were some of the main characters (in a cast of hundreds).

September 22 THE MAN FROM U.N.C.L.E. (NBC). In this international spy series, U.N.C.L.E. (United Network Command for Law and Enforcement) employs agents Napoleon Solo (Robert Vaughn) and Illya Kuryakin (David McCallum) to fight crime syndicate THRUSH.

1964

BEWITCHED (1964). Beautiful, kind witch Samantha (Elizabeth Montgomery) married ad executive Darrin Stephens (Dick York) and moved to the suburbs. Samantha's family, especially mother Endora (Agnes Moorehead), was against her marrying a mere mortal and instead wanted her to stay true to her witchy ways, which mostly consisted of "pranks" to get what she wanted.

CANDID CAMERA was created by Allen Funt (at right) who, along with Durward Kirby, led unsuspecting people through various humorous situations that were filmed with hidden cameras. The puzzled participants were finally let in on the joke when told to "Smile, you're on Candid Camera!"

September 24 THE MUNSTERS (CBS). Herman Munster (Fred Gwynne), Lily Munster (Yvonne DeCarlo), Grandpa Munster (Al Lewis), Eddie Munster (Butch Patrick), Marilyn Munster (Beverly Owen). In this comedy, the family of friendly Frankenstein/Dracula-like "monsters" (who consider themselves normal) live at 1313 Mockingbird Lane in the town of Mockingbird Heights and inter-act in odd ways with their neighbors.

THE MUNSTERS. Six-foot-ten-inch Herman Munster was only one of the weird Munster family. Beautiful Marilyn Munster was considered the misfit. Here we see Grandpa (upside down), Lily, and Herman.

PETTICOAT JUNCTION was the top-ranked new show for 1963. It followed on the heels of other shows with rural settings. *Junction* was set in Hooterville, the end-of-the-line stop for the Cannonball train. Much of the plot centered around Kate Bradley's three marriageable daughters. Kate ran the Shady Rest Hotel in town.

September 25 GOMER PYLE, U.S.M.C. (CBS). Spin off of *The Andy Griffith Show*. In this military comedy series, Pvt. Gomer Pyle (Jim Nabors) from Mayberry, N.C., joined the Marines and served at Camp Henderson, Calif., with Sgt. Vince Carter (Frank Sutton). **September 26 GILLIGAN'S ISLAND** (CBS). Shipwrecked Gilligan (Bob Denver), The Skipper Jonas Gumby (Alan Hale, Jr.), Thurston Howell III (Jim Backus), (Mrs.) Lovey Howell (Natalie Schafer), Ginger Grant (Tina Louise), The Professor Roy Hinkley (Russell Johnson), Mary Ann Summers (Dawn Wells). How they managed to survive for years on an isolated island is a TV mystery. **1965 September 17 THE SMOTHERS BROTHERS SHOW** (CBS). On this clever and intelligent comedy show, Tom Smothers and Dick Smothers played themselves. **September 17 HOGAN'S HEROES** (CBS). Comedy set in Stalag 13, a World War II POW camp, run by inept German Col. Wilhelm Klink (Werner Klemperer) who matched wits with the clever American Col. Robert Hogan (Bob Crane). Hogan marshalled his prisoners so that they could pass information to the Allies and also do such things as make counterfeit money.

I DREAM OF JEANNIE. The wedding of Jeannie (Barbara Eden), a 2,000-year-old genie, and astronaut Tony Nelson (Larry Hagman) in a 1969 episode was the culmination of a long comic saga of love, jealousy, and belief in things that are not quite what they seem.

Based on Grace Metalious' best seller of the same name, PEYTON PLACE (a New England town) was the first soap opera to run successfully in evening hours. Here are Allison MacKenzie (Mia Farrow) and Rodney Harrington (Ryan O'Neal).

One of TV's multitalented geniuses, Steve Allen, seen here with two other outstanding comic talents, Louis Nye and Tim Conway, in a skit on THE STEVE ALLEN SHOW in 1967.

THE BEVERLY HILLBILLIES. The Clampett family, hillbillies from the Ozarks, moved to Beverly Hills (next door to the prominent Drysdales) after oil ("Texas Tea") was discovered in their front yard and they became millionaires.

September 18 I DREAM OF JEANNIE (NBC). Jeannie (Barbara Eden), Astronaut Tony Nelson (Larry Hagman), Capt. Roger Healey (Bill Daily), Psychiatrist Dr. Alfred Bellows (Hayden Rorke), Melissa Stone (Karen Sharpe). Tony lands on a desert island after a space accident and meets Jeannie, a 2,000-year-old genie. Tony returns to the U.S. and tells his tale but no one believes him. He becomes engaged to Melissa and jealous Jeannie (also in love with him) creates havoc to break up the match. Tony's buddy Roger finally believes in Jeannie and her magic powers. Tony realizes he is in love with Jeannie and marries her in a 1969 episode. **1966**

September 8 STAR TREK (NBC). Capt. James T. Kirk (William Shatner), half Earthling/half Vulcan pointy-eared logical Mr. Spock (Leonard Nimoy), Dr. Leonard "Bones" McCoy (DeForest Kelley), Sulu (George Takei), Lt. Uhura (Nichelle Nichols), Engineer Montgomery "Scotty" Scott (James Doohan). Aboard the *U.S.S. Enterprise* in the 23rd century A.D., the crew clad in very unfuturistic space uniforms encountered alien life forms (especially the Romulons and the Klingons) with whom they did battle but learned to understand. "Trekkies" (fans of the show) were fanatically involved with the series.

On air from 1966 to 1971, THAT GIRL was Ann Marie (Marlo Thomas), who lived in New York, took a series of odd jobs, and wanted to be an actress. The comedy also featured boyfriend Don Hollinger (Ted Bessell).

"Your mission, if you should choose to accept it, is......" MISSION: IMPOSSIBLE (1966). A voice on a tape (that "will self-destruct in five seconds") laid out a mission involving a top-secret plan; a puff of smoke from the tape began each week's episode. The highly skilled team of agents managed week after week to solve the difficult international cases.

DARK SHADOWS (1966). A day-time soap with a twist. Although it took place in small-town Maine, it was in the spooky world of vampires and ghost-inhabited houses. Here we see Barnabas Collins (Jonathan Frid) as the 200-year-old vampire.

Host Monty Hall with a contestant on LET'S MAKE A DEAL. Audience members (usually dressed in silly costumes) were able to trade items they had brought with them for hidden prizes, which ranged from worthless "zonks" to highly valuable winnings.

THE CAROL BURNETT SHOW. Singer, dancer, comedian, actor Burnett was the star of a long-running variety/comedy series with a brilliant ensemble cast that included Harvey Korman (left) and Tim Conway. The cast delighted in making each other, as well as the audience, laugh .

THE SMOTHERS BROTHERS, here in 1968, were Tom and Dick Smothers. Their comedy/variety show featured controversial skits and finally was taken off the air because of problems with censors.

1966

September 8 THAT GIRL (ABC). Ann Marie (Marlo Thomas), a young actress left home to find work in New York. While landing a few roles, she worked as a salesgirl or as an office temp. Journalist Don Hollinger (Ted Bessell) was her love interest. One of the first shows to have an independent single young woman as the star. **September 17 MISSION: IMPOSSIBLE** (CBS). Daniel Briggs (Steven Hill), Jim Phelps (Peter Graves, '67), Cinnamon Carter (Barbara Bain), Rollin Hand (Martin Landau), Barney Collier (Greg Morris), Willie Armitage (Peter Lupus). Bob Johnson's voice was heard on the weekly tape laying out the mission for the elite special agents.

Sally Field as lighter-than-air Sister Bertrille, THE FLYING NUN, somewhere over her Convent San Tanco in Puerto Rico.

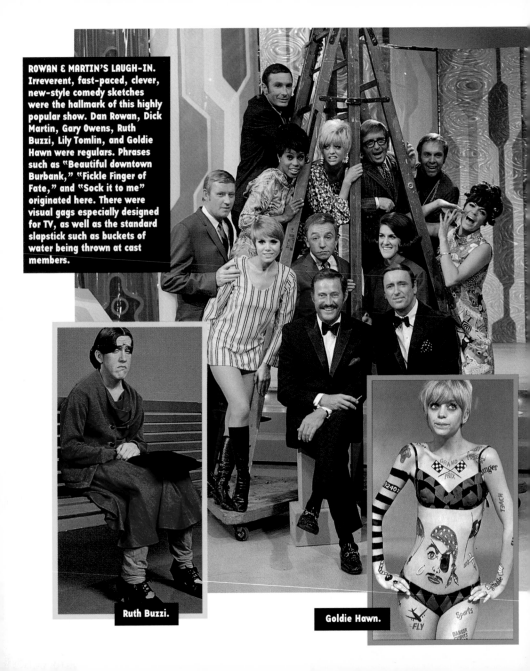

ROWAN & MARTIN'S LAUGH-IN. Irreverent, fast-paced, clever, new-style comedy sketches were the hallmark of this highly popular show. Dan Rowan, Dick Martin, Gary Owens, Ruth Buzzi, Lily Tomlin, and Goldie Hawn were regulars. Phrases such as "Beautiful downtown Burbank," "Fickle Finger of Fate," and "Sock it to me" originated here. There were visual gags especially designed for TV, as well as the standard slapstick such as buckets of water being thrown at cast members.

Ruth Buzzi.

Goldie Hawn.

October 17 (daytime) **January 12, 1968** (prime time). **HOLLYWOOD SQUARES** (NBC). Peter Marshall emcee with Wally Cox and Cliff Arquette. Tic, Tac, Toe with celebrities in each square. There were two contestants to judge the veracity of the answer to a celebritiy's question, which was more-often-than-not a silly one. **1967**

February 5 THE SMOTHERS BROTHERS COMEDY HOUR (CBS). Tom and Dick Smothers hosted a controversial comedy/variety that lampooned all aspects of contemporary life, including the "sacred" ones of motherhood, religion, war, and politics. The ensuing furor became too much for the network, which cancelled the show in 1969 even though ratings were high.

September 11 THE CAROL BURNETT SHOW (CBS). Starring Carol Burnett, Harvey Korman, Lyle Waggoner, Vicki Lawrence, Tim Conway. A highly successful variety/comedy show with a versatile ensemble cast. A guest star appeared each week. Sketches included "Ed and Eunice" (which became the series *Mama's Family*), "Mr. Tudball and Mrs. Wiggins," and "As the Stomach Turns." **1968** TV sets are in 98 percent of U.S. homes.

60 MINUTES was the first news-magazine format show that covered topics ranging from politics to coverups to industrial disasters to lighter fare such as fashion. Here are Mike Wallace and Harry Reasoner, who were with the show from its inception.

VINCENT PRICE   KAREN VALENTINE   DEMOND WILSON

NORMAN FELL   PAUL LYNDE

NANETTE FABRAY

Tic, Tac, Toe with celebrities in each square was the format for HOLLYWOOD SQUARES. Two contestants would judge the veracity of the celeb's answer to a question (usually silly). The contestant "won" the square if he/she guessed correctly. Celebrity banter was the draw.

January 22 ROWAN & MARTIN'S LAUGH-IN (NBC). Dan Rowan, Dick Martin, Gary Owens, Ruth Buzzi. Irreverent comedy sketches, fast-paced, clever. Actors became associated with specific characters. Lily Tomlin's telephone operator originated here; Goldie Hawn's silly blonde; among others. **April 4 MARTIN LUTHER KING, JR., ASSASSINATION** coverage (CBS). **July 15 ONE LIFE TO LIVE** (ABC). Daytime soap still on the air. Even though set in small-town Llanview, the plots still manage to involve a surprisingly varied group of people and fantasy elements. **September 24 60 MINUTES** (CBS). That 60-minute clock is still ticking. Serious investigative reporting has been the hallmark of the show from its inception. **September 26 HAWAII FIVE-O** (CBS). Steve McGarrett (Jack Lord) headed the group of special police in Honolulu. Danny Williams (James MacArthur), Chin Ho Kelly (Kam Fong). The series, filmed on location, had the agents fighting underworld crime bosses. **1969 June 15 HEE HAW** (CBS/syndicated). Roy Clark and Buck Owens, hosts. Frequent guest artists and newcomers played top-notch music and spoke silly one-line jokes in a cornfield setting. There were also skits. Audiences tuned in, although critics panned it.

HEE HAW. Roy Clark and Buck Owens hosted this country music variety/comedy that featured a laughing donkey who provided the "hee, haw." In this unusual format, top-notch country music was alternated with goofy jokes.

THE BRADY BUNCH. Widow Carol (Florence Henderson) with three daughters marries widower Mike Brady (Robert Reed) with three sons to form a solid American family with the help of housekeeper Alice Nelson (Ann B. Davis), who kept the family in line. The show has become a cult classic.

July 20-21 APOLLO 11 WITH THE FIRST HUMANS TO LAND ON THE MOON. (all networks). "The Eagle has landed" as 600 million watch it on TV. **September 14 THE BILL COSBY SHOW** (NBC). Characters are high school phys ed teacher and coach Chet Kinkaid (Bill Cosby), mother Rose Kinkaid (Lillian Randolph), brother Brian Kinkaid (Lee Weaver), sister-in-law Verna Kinkaid (Olga James). This gentle comedy is set in an L.A. working-class high school. **September 23 MARCUS WELBY, M.D.** (ABC). In this top-rated show, Dr. Marcus Welby (Robert Young) is a kind GP in Santa Monica, California, assisted by Dr. Steven Kiley (James Brolin). The doctors become involved in the medical dilemmas and the private lives of their patients. **September 26 THE BRADY BUNCH** (ABC). The American home formed from the all-girl family of widow Carol (Florence Henderson) and all-son family of widower Mike Brady (Robert Reed). The children were Marcia (Maureen McCormick), Jan (Eve Plumb), Cindy (Susan Olsen), Greg (Barry Williams), Peter (Christopher Knight), Bobby (Michael Lookinland). Mike was an architect and the family lived in a large house that also accommodated housekeeper Alice Nelson (Ann B. Davis).

THE PARTRIDGE FAMILY. Shirley (Shirley Jones) and her five children (including Jones' real-life stepson David Cassidy) formed a singing group that traveled cross-country in a painted schoolbus. The show's actors became successful recording artists, especially Cassidy (bottom right), who was a teen idol.

In **HAWAII FIVE-O**, Steve McGarrett (Jack Lord) headed a group of a special branch of the Hawaiian State Police that battled underworld crime. They were based in the Iolani Palace in Honolulu and reported directly to the governor of Hawaii. The series was filmed on location—a big draw for viewers.

MARCUS WELBY, M.D. One of the gentle medical shows. Dr. Marcus Welby (Robert Young) was a GP assisted by Dr. Steven Kiley (James Brolin).

A groundbreaking comedy, THE MARY TYLER MOORE SHOW, showed a successful single career woman working for Lou Grant (Ed Asner) as an assistant producer of a TV news broadcast. Pictured here are Asner, Moore, Ted Knight, and Gavin MacLeod.

ALL IN THE FAMILY, a sitcom starring Carroll O'Connor, Jean Stapleton, Rob Reiner, and Sally Struthers as the working-class Bunker family from Queens, New York, was considered a controversial lightning rod for discussions of society's ills. Archie Bunker was the opinionated head of the household who held forth with his views on racial minorities, women, men who did "women's work," men who didn't work and women who did. Until 1971 when this series premiered, these were not topics for prime-time TV.

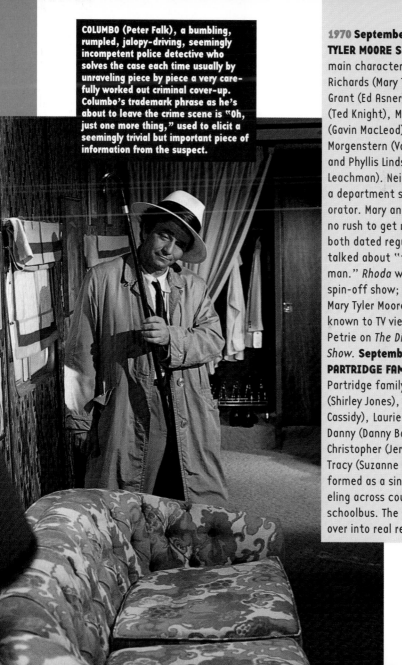

COLUMBO (Peter Falk), a bumbling, rumpled, jalopy-driving, seemingly incompetent police detective who solves the case each time usually by unraveling piece by piece a very carefully worked out criminal cover-up. Columbo's trademark phrase as he's about to leave the crime scene is "Oh, just one more thing," used to elicit a seemingly trivial but important piece of information from the suspect.

1970 September 19 THE MARY TYLER MOORE SHOW (CBS). The main characters were: Mary Richards (Mary Tyler Moore), Lou Grant (Ed Asner), Ted Baxter (Ted Knight), Murray Slaughter (Gavin MacLeod), Rhoda Morgenstern (Valerie Harper), and Phyllis Lindstrom (Cloris Leachman). Neighbor Rhoda was a department store window decorator. Mary and Rhoda showed no rush to get married, although both dated regularly and Rhoda talked about "finding the right man." *Rhoda* was a successful spin-off show; as was *Phyllis*. Mary Tyler Moore had been well known to TV viewers as Laura Petrie on *The Dick Van Dyke Show*. **September 25 THE PARTRIDGE FAMILY** (ABC). The Partridge family: mother Shirley (Shirley Jones), Keith (David Cassidy), Laurie (Susan Dey), Danny (Danny Bonaduce), Christopher (Jeremy Gelbwaks), Tracy (Suzanne Crough), all performed as a singing group traveling across country in a painted schoolbus. The show crossed over into real recording success.

M*A*S*H (for Mobile Army Surgical Hospital), which began its run in 1972, was based on the 1970 film by Robert Altman. It was set during the Korean War, but most viewers recognized that it really was as much about the then-raging Vietnam conflict.

1971 **January 12 ALL IN THE FAMILY** (CBS). Archie Bunker (Carroll O'Conner), Edith Bunker (Jean Stapleton), Gloria Stivic (Sally Struthers), Mike Stivic (Rob Reiner). "Those Were the Days" was the lead-in song. At times considered a lightning rod for discussions of society's ills, the controversial comedy show became a top hit. Archie Bunker was a blue-collar, predjudiced, opinionated head of household who played off against unpreju- diced wife Edith and very liberal son-in-law Mike ("Meathead"). **September 15 COLUMBO** (NBC). Lt. Columbo as portrayed by Peter Falk is a seemingly incom- petent police detective, but solves the case each time. **1972** **September 14 THE WALTONS** (CBS). A Depression-era family drama centering on the Waltons. The series was thought to have little chance of success in its first season, but it stayed on air from 1972 to '81. **September 16 THE BOB NEWHART SHOW** (CBS). Bob Newhart in his second suc- cessful show. His first, which was also called *The Bob Newhart Show* (it ran from 1961 to 1962), featured Newhart as a stand-up comedian, who created most of his long monologues over the telephone.

THE BOB NEWHART SHOW featured Bob Hartley (stand-up comedian Newhart), a psychologist, and his wife Emily (Suzanne Pleshette), a schoolteacher. Secretary Carol (Marcia Wallace) worked for both Bob and Jerry (Peter Bonerz), a dentist. Plots centered around home, office, Bob's patients, either singly or in group therapy sessions, and wacky neighbor Howard Borden (Bill Daily), who always showed up at mealtime.

October 14 KUNG FU (ABC). Buddhist monk Kwai Chang Caine (David Carradine) grew up in China in the 1850s as an orphan raised by monks who taught him kung fu. After killing a member of the Chinese royal family, he fled to the American West. Master Po (Keye Luke) and Master Kan (Philip Ahn) were his often-quoted Chinese teachers seen in flashbacks to his youth. Camera techniques and sparse dialogue helped make the stories unusual. **1973 October 24 KOJAK** (CBS). Lt. Theo Kojak (Telly Savalas), Frank McNeil (Dan Frazer), Lt. Bobby Crocker (Kevin Dobson), Detective Stavros (George Savalas).

THE WALTONS. This Depression-era drama had very low ratings in its first season, but rose to second after *All in the Family* in the second season. It also garnered numerous awards, including a few Emmys.

"Well, We're Movin' On Up." **THE JEFFERSONS**, a spin-off of *All in the Family*, featured neighbors of the Bunkers who, after running a successful dry cleaning business, moved from Queens to a luxury high-rise in the upper east side of Manhattan.

Kojak reported to McNeil, his ex-partner, working New York's Manhattan South area. Kojak's trademark was a lollipop he often had in his mouth. **1974 January 15 HAPPY DAYS** (ABC). A hit—once the cool character the "Fonz" (Henry Winkler) was highlighted in the second season. The show featured Richie Cunningham (Ron Howard) and Potsie Weber (Anson Williams) as two Jefferson High School students. "Happy Days" the song became a hit. **January 18 THE SIX MILLION DOLLAR MAN** (ABC). Col. Steve Austin (Lee Majors) was an astronaut injured in a test vehicle crash. Dr. Rudy Wells (Alan Oppenheimer), a government physician, pioneered a new operation—the replacement of damaged human parts with super "bionic" elements that endowed the Colonel with extraordinary powers. Austin, a new superhero, completed numerous missions for the Office of Scientific Information working under the direction of Oscar Goldman (Richard Anderson). In the second season, Jaime Somers (Lindsay Wagner), the *Bionic Woman*, was introduced (leading to a spin-off show).

THE MALE-DOMINATED HERO SHOWS OF THE 1970S

BARETTA. Tony Baretta (Robert Blake) is a street smart, rough-on-the-outside, nice-on-the-inside detective who often worked undercover (in trademark bluejeans and a T-shirt). The popular theme song was "Keep Your Eye on the Sparrow," sung by Sammy Davis, Jr.

THE SIX MILLION DOLLAR MAN featured Lee Majors as Col. Steve Austin, an astronaut injured in a test vehicle crash. His damaged body parts were replaced with super atomic-powered elements that endowed the newly recreated Austin with superhero powers of strength, agility, speed, and vision, that enabled him to complete critical missions for the Office of Scientific Information.

THE ROCKFORD FILES. Living in a trailer on a California beach, ex-con P.I. Jim Rockford (James Garner) often takes cases the police think are already solved. He uses fellow ex-cons to help him do the job and get out of close calls. The theme song "The Rockford Files" made the 1975 hit parade.

Lt. Theo KOJAK (Telly Savalas) follows his own rules and reports to his ex-partner Frank O'Neill (Dan Frazer) out of Manhattan South. Despite (or because of) their non-traditional working methods they solve plenty of crimes.

KUNG FU starred David Carradine as Kwai Chang Caine a martial arts expert who used his prodigious skills only when really pushed. Forced to flee China after killing a man, Caine had to give up his way of life as a priest there. The show was notable for its slow-motion sequences showing kung fu moves .

NBC's SATURDAY NIGHT LIVE, one of the all-time great, innovative, outrageous comedy/satire shows. With its repertory company, it created some of the most memorable characters and sketches. Among them are: The Coneheads, The Whiners, The Blues Brothers. "The Not Ready for Prime Time Players" included Chevy Chase ("I'm Chevy Chase, and you're not"), John Belushi (Samurai Warrior), Dan Akroyd, Gilda Radner (Baba Wawa), Garrett Morris, Jane Curtin, Laraine Newman, Albert Brooks. Other actors who came later included: Al Franken, Joe Piscopo, Eddie Murphy, Julia Louis-Dreyfus, Billy Crystal, Martin Short, Dana Carvey, and others. Guest hosts and musical guests were equally legendary. Hosts included people such as Ed Koch, mayor of New York, and other non-TV people. Guest artists included Candice Bergen, Dick Cavett, Elliot Gould, Paul Simon.

Gilda Radner as Roseanne Rosanna-Danna.

Chevy Chase in Weekend Update, a spoof of nightly newscasts.

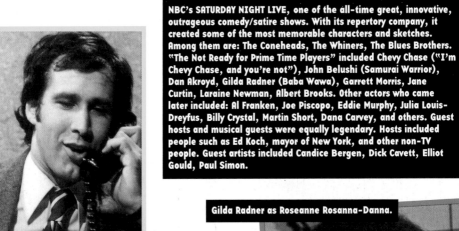

Gilda Radner.

SATURDAY NIGHT LIVE

John Belushi as Samurai Warrior.

Eddie Murphy as Stevie Wonder.

Jane Curtin, Dan Aykroyd, and Laraine Newman as The Coneheads, aliens pretending to be a normal Earth family ("We're from France").

John Travolta

WELCOME BACK, KOTTER. James Buchanan High School in Brooklyn was the setting for this class of "sweathogs" taught by Gabe Kotter (Gabriel Kaplan), who had been a student there himself. John Travolta (here, second from left), who played Vinnie Barbarino, got his big break on this show.

HAPPY DAYS. Another show featuring teenagers, here at Jefferson High School in Milwaukee, was a huge hit once the cool, leather-jacket-wearing, motorcycle-riding "Fonz" (Arthur Fonzarelli, played by Henry Winkler, back right) was given a bigger role in the second season.

July 24-30 House Judiciary Committee **DEBATES ON RICHARD NIXON'S IMPEACHMENT** (all networks). **August 8 NIXON'S RESIGNATION SPEECH** (all networks). **September 13 THE ROCKFORD FILES** (NBC). P.I. Jim Rockford (James Garner), his father Rocky Rockford (Noah Beery), his foe and friend Det. Dennis Becker (Joe Santos), his girlfriend and attorney Beth Davenport (Gretchen Corbett). **September 13 CHICO AND THE MAN** (NBC). Set in an East L.A. barrio, Ed Brown (Jack Albertson) a white owner of the garage in which Mexican-American Chico Rodriguez (Freddie Prinze) works. Prinze died in 1977 at age 22, but the show went on. A very young Gabriel Melgar joined the cast. **1975 January 6 WHEEL OF FORTUNE** (NBC, CBS, syndicated). Game show in which contestants spin a wheel to get letters to complete a mystery word or phrase. Pat Sajak (who began in 1982) is the host most associated with the show along with Vanna White, who turned over the letters and wore a new outfit for each program.

ONE DAY AT A TIME. A divorced mom, Ann Romano (Bonnie Franklin), two teenaged daughters, a love interest for mom, and the super of their building were the core players in this popular sitcom.

S.W.A.T. The Special Weapons and Tactics team was a special police unit working in the state of California. The show was considered one of the most violent of its time.

One of the 1970s police-partners-buddies shows was STARSKY & HUTCH. Det. Dave Starsky (Paul Michael Glaser) and Det. Ken "Hutch" Hutchinson (David Soul) were often found in Starsky's red car solving tough cases in tough neighborhoods.

RHODA (Valerie Harper) was a spin-off of *The Mary Tyler Moore Show*. Rhoda Morgenstern was single (later married and then separated) and living in New York near her sister Brenda (Julie Kavner). They are seen here with Frank Converse.

January 17 BARETTA (ABC). Theme song "Keep Your Eye on the Sparrow" sung by Sammy Davis, Jr. Det. Tony Baretta (Robert Blake), a street-smart detective who often worked undercover. **January 18 THE JEFFERSONS** (CBS). George Jefferson (Sherman Hemsley), Louise Jefferson (Isabel Sanford), Lionel Jefferson (Mike Evans), Helen Willis (Roxie Roker), Tom Willis (Franklin Cover), Florence Johnston, the maid (Marla Gibbs). In this sitcom popular for more than a decade, the Jeffersons were neighbors of Archie Bunker in Queens. Equally bigoted George owns a profitable dry cleaning establishment, allowing the Jeffersons to move to a luxury apartment building on the upper east side of Manhattan. **September 3 STARSKY & HUTCH** (ABC). One of the popular police shows of this period. This fairly violent hour-long drama featured Det. Dave Starsky (Paul Michael Glaser) and Det. Ken "Hutch" Hutchinson (David Soul).

1975

THREE'S COMPANY. Roommates Janet Wood (Joyce DeWitt) and Chrissy Snow (Suzanne Somers) needed a third and took in Jack Tripper (John Ritter). The comedy plots centered on perceived misunderstandings about the relationship among the three, with Jack finally pretending to be homosexual to convince the landlord that nothing immoral was going on. In fact, the roommates were just friends, but the hint of "scandal" was there.

Lindsay Wagner as THE BIONIC WOMAN Jaime Somers, who barely survived a sky-diving accident but was reconstructed better than ever by the same team who pieced together Steve Austin, *The Six Million Dollar Man*. Jaime went on to work along with Austin for the Office of Scientific Information (OSI). The two superheroes were also romantically linked.

Three detectives, the "Angels," who worked mostly undercover for Charlie Townsend (never seen, voice of John Forsythe). CHARLIE'S ANGELS launched the career of Farrah Fawcett-Majors (center, as Jill Munroe). Others of the beautiful but tough team were Kate Jackson (as Sabrina Duncan) and Jaclyn Smith (as Kelly Garrett). Later recruits included Cheryl Ladd. The detectives were placed in situations that allowed them to work in bathing suits and other revealing clothing.

September 9 WELCOME BACK, KOTTER (ABC). Theme song "Welcome Back" composed and sung by John Sebastian. James Buchanan High School was the setting for this class of "sweat-hogs"—difficult students—taught by Gabe Kotter (Gabriel Kaplan). Students Vinnie Barbarino (John Travolta), Juan Luis Pedro Phillipo de Huevos Epstein, known just as Epstein (Robert Hegyes), "Boom Boom" Washington (Lawrence-Hilton Jacobs), Arnold Horshack (Ron Palillo) provided the tough-talk humor and pace. The show was created by Alan Sacks and Gabriel Kaplan, who himself had been a student like the ones portrayed. **October 11 SATURDAY NIGHT LIVE** (NBC). Original sharp ridiculous up-to-the-minute

LAVERNE & SHIRLEY (Penny Marshall and Cindy Williams) were first seen on Happy Days when they had blind dates with Richie and the Fonz. They worked on an assembly line in a bottle cap factory and dreamed of getting ahead.

spoofs of everything from the nightly news to commercials. **December 16 ONE DAY AT A TIME** (CBS). Ann Romano Royer (Bonnie Franklin), 17-year-old daughter Julie Cooper Horvath (Mackenzie Phillips), 15-year-old daughter Barbara Cooper Royer (Valerie Bertinelli), the building super Schneider (Pat Harrington, Jr.), love interest David Kane (Richard Masur). Divorced Ann Romano lived with her two daughters in Indianapolis.

MORK & MINDY. Mork (Robin Williams), an alien from the planet Ork, lands on Earth in a giant eggshell near Boulder, Colorado. He had been sent away from Ork because he was too funny and was told to study the "strange" Earthlings. When he landed, Mindy Beth McConnell (Pam Dawber) befriended him and let him stay in her attic. Mork signed off each show with "Na nu na nu" (Orkan "goodnight"). Williams' amazing comedic and linguistic talents carried the show and made it hugely popular.

1976 January MARY HARTMAN, MARY HARTMAN (syndicated). Considered too controversial for network television, this satire of TV soaps was picked up by local stations for late-night viewing. Mary Hartman (Louise Lasser) lived in Fernwood, Ohio, and was serious about facing the perils of housework as portrayed in TV commercials. There were all of the regular soap scenarios, but played here with a spin. Husband Tom (Greg Mullvaney) was impotent; Mary had an affair with a policeman; daughter Heather (Claudia Lamb) was kidnapped by terrorists; her friend Loretta Haggers (Mary Kay Place) was paralyzed; and so on.

FANTASY ISLAND. Island owner Mr. Roarke (Ricardo Montalban) and his assistant Tattoo (Herve Villechaize) welcomed guests to the island for a one-week dream come true. There was often a "magic" quality to the episodes. "Boss, the plane, the plane..." was how Tattoo announced the arrival of the guests.

THE LOVE BOAT (1977-86) was filmed during real sailings of the *Pacific Princess* cruise ship. The crew was headed by Captain Merrill Stubing (Gavin MacLeod) and included Dr. Adam Bricker (Bernie Kopell), Purser "Gopher" Smith (Fred Grandy, who later became a congressman), bartender Isaac Washington (Ted Lange), cruise director Julie McCoy (Lauren Tewes). Guest appearances were made by numerous stars including Andy Warhol, Steve Allen, Janet Gaynor, and Pearl Bailey.

HART TO HART starred Robert Wagner as Jonathan Hart (a rich businessman) and Stephanie Powers as Jennifer Hart (a writer), amateur detectives who often traveled to exotic locations and solved cases with the help of their chauffeur, Max, and dog, Freeway. The show was fast paced and breezy.

TAXI. The Sunshine Cab Company in New York was run by tyrant dispatcher Louie De Palma (Danny DeVito). His drivers included Alex Reiger (Judd Hirsch), art gallery receptionist Elaine Nardo (Marilu Henner), and boxer Tony Banta (Tony Danza), among others. The linguistic mystery mechanic Latka Gravas was played by the brilliant performance artist Andy Kaufman.

THE JACK BENNY SHOW, August 23, 1977. Mel Blanc "the man of a thousand voices" here as Professor Le Blanc, gives violin lessons to Jack Benny.

1976

January 14 THE BIONIC WOMAN (ABC; then NBC). A spin-off of *The Six Million Dollar Man*, Jaime Somers was reconstructed and, as the Bionic Woman, went on to become a superhero teacher and undercover agent for the government's Office of Scientific Information. OSI chief Oscar Goldman (Richard Anderson) and doctor-in-charge-of-bionic-operations Dr. Rudy Wells (Martin Brooks) appeared on both shows.

THE DUKES OF HAZZARD (1979–85). Set "east of the Mississippi, south of the Ohio" in Hazzard County, the show featured good ol' boys and girls and a car, "The General Lee," a Dodge Charger entered through the windows. Luke (Tom Wopat) and Bo Duke (John Schneider), and cousin Daisy (Catherine Bach) tried to outwit corrupt politician "Boss" Hogg (Sorell Brooke) and, often, Sheriff Coltrane (James Best) as well. Uncle Jesse Duke (Denver Pyle) helped keep the rambunctious family together.

GENERAL HOSPITAL. On air in 1963, it is still going. This daytime soap is one of TV's most successful. The wedding of Luke (Tony Geary) and Laura (Genie Francis) from the 1981 season was one of the most-watched daytime episodes ever.

A two-season sitcom (1980-82), BOSOM BUDDIES featured two guys in drag. Roommates Henry Desmond (Peter Scolari) and Kip Wilson (Tom Hanks) lost their apartment and had to move into the Susan B. Anthony Residence for Women, thus the female attire.

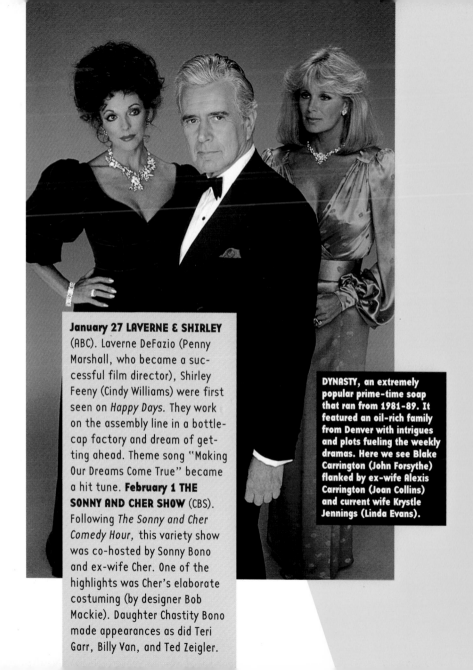

January 27 LAVERNE & SHIRLEY
(ABC). Laverne DeFazio (Penny
Marshall, who became a successful film director), Shirley
Feeny (Cindy Williams) were first
seen on *Happy Days*. They work
on the assembly line in a bottle-
cap factory and dream of getting ahead. Theme song "Making
Our Dreams Come True" became
a hit tune. **February 1 THE
SONNY AND CHER SHOW** (CBS).
Following *The Sonny and Cher
Comedy Hour,* this variety show
was co-hosted by Sonny Bono
and ex-wife Cher. One of the
highlights was Cher's elaborate
costuming (by designer Bob
Mackie). Daughter Chastity Bono
made appearances as did Teri
Garr, Billy Van, and Ted Zeigler.

**DYNASTY, an extremely
popular prime-time soap
that ran from 1981-89. It
featured an oil-rich family
from Denver with intrigues
and plots fueling the weekly
dramas. Here we see Blake
Carrington (John Forsythe)
flanked by ex-wife Alexis
Carrington (Joan Collins)
and current wife Krystle
Jennings (Linda Evans).**

September THE MUPPET SHOW (syndicated). Kermit the Frog first appeared on American TV in 1957 on *The Steve Allen Show*. Created by Jim Henson, the Muppets (a cross between puppets and marionettes) are international classics that later starred on *Sesame Street*. Chief Muppeteers: Jim Henson, Frank Oz, Richard Hunt, Dave Goelz, Jerry Nelson. Kermit hosts the show; among the players are Miss Piggy, a glamorous, determined pig; Rowlf, a dog who plays the piano; Swedish Chef; Gonzo, a master of odd stunts; Fozzie Bear, a comic who gets the "hook" each time.

September 22 CHARLIE'S ANGELS (ABC). This was probably the most popular show of this season. The hour-long detective show launched Farrah Fawcett-Majors who played Jill Munroe, one of the "Angels." Fawcett-Majors left the show in 1977 and Cheryl Ladd joined during the next season. **1977 January 23 ROOTS** (ABC). The most watched TV drama in history (over 130 million viewers). Eight-night special based on Alex Haley's book *Roots*, it is the story of

A female police-detective-partners "buddy" show, CAGNEY & LACEY featured single Det. Chris Cagney (Sharon Gless) and married mother Det. Mary Beth Lacey (Tyne Daly), who mostly worked undercover.

Kunta Kinte, a young boy born in Gambia and then sent into slavery; it traces his descendants and others up to present-day U.S. The star-filled cast included Le Var Burton (Kinte as a youth), John Amos (Kinte grown), Cicely Tyson, Maya Angelou, O.J. Simpson, Moses Gunn, Hari Rhodes, Edward Asner, Louis Gossett, Jr., Lorne Greene, Vic Morrow, Robert Reed, Sandy Duncan, Leslie Uggams, George Hamilton, Lillian Randolph, Ben Vereen, Lloyd Bridges, Richard Roundtree, Scatman Crothers, Burl Ives, and others.

CHEERS, the Boston bar "where everybody knows your name." Bartender Sam Malone (Ted Danson) is an ex-pitcher for the Boston Red Sox and recovered alcoholic who is in an on-again, off-again relationship with complicated, college-educated Diane Chambers (Shelley Long).

HILL STREET BLUES, a police drama set in a run-down area of a large city, influenced the style of future police shows with its realistic dialogue and choppy pacing of camera shots. Here in a tense moment in an episode called "Watt a Way to Go" are Lt. Henry Goldblume (Joe Spano), Officer Bobby Hill (Michael Warren), and Officer Andy Renko (Charles Haid).

HILL STREET BLUES. Public Defender Joyce Davenport (Veronica Hamel) and Capt. Frank Furillo (Daniel J. Travanti) were secretly lovers and then married.

March 15 THREE'S COMPANY (ABC). Roommates Janet Wood and Chrissy Snow needed a third and they took in Jack Tripper. Plots centered on misunderstandings about the relationship of the three. **September 13 SOAP** (ABC). Prime-time controversial spoof on soap operas. All of the convoluted plot twists and undercurrents of sex, murder, scandal, and aliens were here. The rich family Tate and the working-class family Campbell were the center of the stories. **September 24 THE LOVE BOAT** (ABC). Set on the cruise ship *Pacific Princess,* which took aboard a new set of guest/passengers for each episode. The crew appeared regularly and guest appearances were made by numerous stars.

ST. ELSEWHERE is one of the grittier hospital dramas. Set at St. Eligius Hospital (St. Elsewhere) run by Chief Dr. Donald Westphall (Ed Flanders), the series featured crises of conscience, affairs, suicides, and humor—and, of course, operating room drama. The strange final episode revealed that Tommy, an autistic child, had imagined everything while contemplating a snow globe.

LATE NIGHT WITH DAVID LETTERMAN ran on NBC from 1982 to 1993 in the 12:30 A.M. time slot following *The Tonight Show*. Here Letterman interviews "shock jock" Howard Stern and movie star Tom Cruise. Letterman was notable for displaying a sophisticated sense of television as a medium, walking up to the camera, pacing, turning images upside down. His show was irreverent and innovative.

1978 January 28 FANTASY ISLAND (ABC). Island owner Mr. Roarke (Ricardo Montalban) and his assistant Tattoo (Herve Villechaize) welcomed guests to the island for a one-week dream life come true. Guests could be a shy person who became popular, a poor one who saw wealth, or someone who wanted respect and love and found it. Often there was a "magic" quality to the episodes.

Jay Leno became the successor to Johnny Carson as host of THE TONIGHT SHOW. Once Letterman moved to CBS he went head-to-head with Leno in the same time slot. Leno is seen here with guest Julia Roberts.

WHO'S THE BOSS? (1984), a sitcom about Tony Micelli (Tony Danza), a widower and former St. Louis Cardinals baseball player, who moves with his daughter Samantha (Alyssa Milano) to be house-keeper to Angela Bower (Judith Light) and her young son Jonathan (Dany Pintauro). Tony pulls the household together. Although Tony and Angela date other people, their own relationship begins to grow. In later episodes, Tony goes to college and Angela starts her own advertising agency.

FAMILY TIES (NBC). In this family comedy, Alex (Michael J. Fox) is the eldest and conservative (he loves Richard Nixon and reads the *Wall Street Journal*) son in the Keaton family of Columbus, Ohio. Mallory (Justine Bateman), his younger sister, is not quite so intellectual. Jennifer (Tina Youthers) is the youngest in the family.

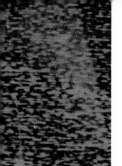

April 2 DALLAS (CBS). A popular night-time soap opera (running until 1991) set among the oil rich of Dallas, Texas. The Ewing family lived at seemingly enormous Southfork Ranch (still hardly big enough to contain all the schemes and plot twists). Played masterfully by Larry Hagman as J.R. Ewing, the eldest son of Miss Ellie (Barbara Bel Geddes) and Jock Ewing (Jim Davis), brother to Bobby (Patrick Duffy). J.R. is married to Sue Ellen (Linda Grey), Bobby to Pam (Victoria Principal). Plots revolved around sex, oil wealth, revenge, mostly focusing on J.R.'s lack of conscience. Flashy fashion and unending family conflicts added further interest. One of the most widely followed TV series all over the globe. "Who shot J.R.?" was the season finale cliffhanger in 1980 and was the second most watched episode in TV history (the culprit was sister-in-law Kristen; J.R. lived and Kristen was never prosecuted).

THE COSBY SHOW featured family values for the 1980s. Two professionals, obstetrician Dr. Cliff Huxtable (Bill Cosby) and lawyer Clair (Phylicia Ayers-Allen Rashad) were parents to four children. Scenes centered around family life.

WEBSTER (played by Emmanuel Lewis) was a seven-year-old orphan taken in by George Papadopolis (Alex Karras) and his wife Katherine Calder-Young (Susan Clark).

THE A TEAM. This group of four Vietnam vets, including B.A. Barracus (played by Mr. T), was for hire to anyone who could pay their fee.

fashionable and very very rich in-love couple ("when they met it was murder") are detectives who travel widely and in style to solve mysteries. **September 23 TRAPPER JOHN, M.D.** (CBS). "Trapper John," Dr. John McIntyre (Pernell Roberts), "Gonzo," Dr. George Alonzo Gates (Gregory Harrison), "Starch," Nurse Clara Willoughby (Mary McCarty), "Ripples," Nurse Gloria Brancusi (Christopher Norris). Trapper John (a character on *M*A*S*H*) is head of surgery at San Francisco Memorial Hospital. Much younger Gonzo works with him and they circumvent various hospital rules to better serve their patients.

September 12 TAXI (ABC). The Sunshine Cab Company was where a group of New Yorkers worked. Tyrant Louie De Palma (Danny DeVito) oversaw driving assignments from high above the garage floor. **September 14 MORK & MINDY** (ABC). Spin-off of *Happy Days*. Mork, from planet Ork, landed on Earth near Boulder, Colorado. When he landed, Mindy let him stay in the attic of her apartment house. Later years saw Mork and Mindy marry and give birth to a 225-pound Jonathan Winters who, as was the Orkan way, grew younger each year. 1979 **September 22 HART TO HART** (ABC). Created by Sidney Sheldon. Jonathan and Jennifer Hart, a

TOUGH GUYS

MacGYVER (Richard Dean Anderson) was a problem-solving secret agent who worked for Phoenix Foundation, which helped out government agencies. Unlike other agent-heroes, MacGyver relied on ingenuity rather than on weapons to complete his missions.

MIAMI VICE was the first MTV-generation cop show. The rhythm of the film cuts, the music, the stylish pastel-colored clothing, the fast Ferrari, fast boats, and the backdrop of Miami Beach created a show in which it was sexy to watch cops chase the bad guys. The detective partners were "Sonny" Crockett (Don Johnson) and Ricardo Tubbs (Philip Michael Thomas).

L.A. LAW was a dramatic series that dealt with up-to-the-minute legal/social issues in a high-powered law firm with soap-opera plot twists. Here are lawyer Michael Kuzak (Harry Hamlin) and Assistant D.A. Grace Van Owen (Susan Dey), who were two of the romantic leads on the show.

TRAPPER JOHN, M.D. In this October 1985 episode, Dr. "Trapper" McIntyre (Pernell Roberts) examines patient Jack Dearborne (guest star Hoyt Axton), who is about to undergo an artificial heart transplant. The character of Trapper first appeared on M*A*S*H.

December 27 KNOTS LANDING (CBS). Spin-off of *Dallas*. Weak, former alcoholic Gary Ewing (Ted Shackelford) and his wife twice over, Valene Ewing (Joan Van Ark), moved to Knots Landing in southern California to get away from the scheming Ewings of Dallas. Divorce, murder, affairs, drugs, alcohol, lust—and sometimes visits from the other Ewing brothers of Dallas—are all plot elements. **1980 November 27 BOSOM BUDDIES** (ABC). In this guys-dressed-as-girls-and-only-one-person-knows-their-true-identity comedy, the Susan B. Anthony Residence for Women was the locale where Henry Desmond (Peter Scolari) became Hildegarde and Kip Wilson (Tom Hanks) became Buffy, two "females," so that they could share cheap housing with Amy Cassidy (Wendie Jo Sperber), one of their co-workers at an advertising agency.

NYPD BLUE is one of the more controversial police dramas very popular with viewers. It features Det. Bobby Simone (Jimmy Smits) and Det. Andy Sipowicz (Dennis Franz). The drama centers on the detective's personal lives as well as on their police work.

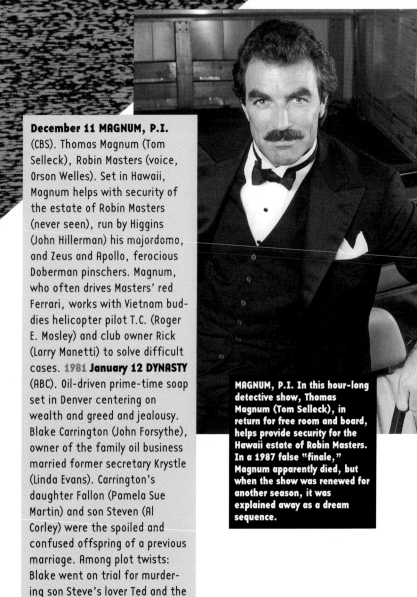

December 11 MAGNUM, P.I.
(CBS). Thomas Magnum (Tom
Selleck), Robin Masters (voice,
Orson Welles). Set in Hawaii,
Magnum helps with security of
the estate of Robin Masters
(never seen), run by Higgins
(John Hillerman) his majordomo,
and Zeus and Apollo, ferocious
Doberman pinschers. Magnum,
who often drives Masters' red
Ferrari, works with Vietnam bud-
dies helicopter pilot T.C. (Roger
E. Mosley) and club owner Rick
(Larry Manetti) to solve difficult
cases. 1981 **January 12 DYNASTY**
(ABC). Oil-driven prime-time soap
set in Denver centering on
wealth and greed and jealousy.
Blake Carrington (John Forsythe),
owner of the family oil business
married former secretary Krystle
(Linda Evans). Carrington's
daughter Fallon (Pamela Sue
Martin) and son Steven (Al
Corley) were the spoiled and
confused offspring of a previous
marriage. Among plot twists:
Blake went on trial for murder-
ing son Steve's lover Ted and the

**MAGNUM, P.I. In this hour-long
detective show, Thomas
Magnum (Tom Selleck), in
return for free room and board,
helps provide security for the
Hawaii estate of Robin Masters.
In a 1987 false "finale,"
Magnum apparently died, but
when the show was renewed for
another season, it was
explained away as a dream
sequence.**

veiled witness was ex-wife Alexis who became the rival of Krystle. **January 15 HILL ST. BLUES** (NBC). Created by Steven Bochco. Police drama set in the Hill Street Station. Capt. Frank Furillo (Daniel J. Travanti) ran the station house with Sgt. Phil Esterhaus (Michael Conrad). Officer Bobby Hill and Officer Andy Renko are partners. Hallmarks were realism captured in the choppy pacing of the camera shots and the dialogue. These elements influenced many other TV dramas.

1986. ALF (Alien Life Form), a cute, fuzzy, wisecracking space creature, crash lands in suburban America on the home of the Tanner family. ALF (whose voice is that of Paul Fusco, one of the creators of the show), from planet Melmac, becomes part of the household. A cartoon version of ALF followed in 1987.

In the 1980s (before Gen-X became hot), yuppies in their 30s were the audience to go after. THIRTYSOME-THING featured two upper-middle-class couples in Philadelphia struggling with the ups and downs of their lives, very much like the target audience for the show.

July 29 WEDDING OF LADY DIANA SPENCER AND PRINCE CHARLES at St. Paul's Cathedral, London (all networks). **August 1 MTV IS LAUNCHED** (cable). Initially only music videos, it influenced the look and rhythm of TV programs, commercials, and fashions. **December 4 FALCON CREST** (CBS). Some of the main characters: manipulative Angela Channing (Jane Wyman), good guy Chase Gioberti (Robert Foxworth), Maggie Gioberti Channing (Susan Sullivan), lazy playboy Lance Cumson (Lorenzo Lamas). Napa Valley Falcon Crest winery ruled by scheming Angela. This soap followed the popular *Dallas*. Bomb plots, schemes, love affairs, power struggles, family feuds—the stuff of classic soap opera—played out on a night-time show in a beautiful northern California setting.

Set in a vineyard in California wine country, FALCON CREST featured Jane Wyman as Angela Channing who plotted to control the winery. In this 1988 episode are Richard Channing (David Selby), an "illegitimate" Channing who has married Maggie Channing (Susan Sullivan), the widow of Angela's nephew, who had been fighting for control of Falcon Crest.

1982 February 2 LATE NIGHT WITH DAVID LETTERMAN (NBC). David Letterman, Paul Shaffer bandleader, Calvert DeForest as Larry "Bud" Melman. This TV talk show turned the medium (sometimes literally) on its head. Letterman played a sophisticated TV game, walking up to the camera, pacing, turning images upside down. Very little about the show was the expected. There were Stupid Pet Tricks, Letterman's Velcro and Alka Seltzer suits, gigantic bowls of

Three men and babies: FULL HOUSE features a widower with children to raise who is joined by his brother-in-law and his closest friend.

MARRIED...WITH CHILDREN. Peg Bundy (Katey Sagal) and husband Al Bundy (Ed O'Neill) are parents of Kelly and Bud—all part of a totally dysfunctional family with few wholesome values. This cartoonish sitcom became an audience favorite despite early negative reviews.

Jello. The show lasted until 1993 when Letterman moved to CBS. **March 25 CAGNEY & LACEY** (CBS). Undercover police detective partners and friends Det. Mary Beth Lacey (Tyne Daly) and Det. Chris Cagney (Meg Foster, then Sharon Gless). Taken off the air due to poor ratings after the first season, viewer mail and phone calls persuaded CBS to try again and the show was a success. **September 16 WEBSTER** (ABC). Created for Emmanuel Lewis (Webster), who shows up on the doorstep of his godfather George Papadapolis (Alex Karras) after his parents are killed in an auto accident and becomes part of the family.

September 30 CHEERS (NBC). The Boston bar. Early regular characters: ex-pitcher for the Boston Red Sox, recovered alcoholic, womanizer, bartender Sam Malone (Ted Danson); fast-talking waitress, single mother Carla Tortelli (Rhea Perlman); college-educated sometime-romantic-interest of Sam's, waitress Diane Chambers (Shelley Long); everyday bar patron, unemployed accountant, married to never-seen Vera, Norm Peterson (George Wendt); mailman with white socks and endless trivia information Cliff Clavin (John Ratzenberger). Later bar patrons included psychiatrist Dr. Frasier Crane (Kelsey Grammer) and his wife psychiatrist Dr. Lilith Sternin Crane (Bebe Neuwirth); bar employees included manager Rebecca Howe (Kirstie Alley); bartender Woody Boyd (Woody Harrelson).

October 26 ST. ELSEWHERE (NBC). Set at Boston's St. Eligius Hospital ("St. Elsewhere"), where the patients are neither rich nor articulate about demanding the latest medical techniques. That's handled by the very competent staff: Chief Dr. Donald Westphall (Ed Flanders), Dr. Mark Craig (William Daniels), Dr. Daniel Auschlander (Norman Lloyd), Dr. Ben Samuels (David Birney), Dr. Cathy Martin (Barbara Whinnery), Dr. Peter White (Terence Knox). There are crises of conscience, affairs, suicides, illness, and humor.

MAUDE (Bea Arthur) was Edith Bunker's liberal, outspoken cousin on *All in the Family* before she became the central character of her own show.

ROSEANNE. One of the most popular family sitcoms. Centered on the realistically blue-collar Conner family with dad Dan (John Goodman) and mom Roseanne (Roseanne) and kids Becky, Darlene, and D.J. who loved each other despite the everyday ups and downs.

THE WONDER YEARS was narrated by Daniel Stern as a grown-up Kevin Arnold (played on screen by Fred Savage, in the middle here), who was looking back to his years in suburban John F. Kennedy Junior High School beginning in 1968. In this 1988 shot we see Paul Pfeiffer (Josh Saviano), Kevin's friend, and "Winnie" Cooper (Danica McKellar), his sometime girlfriend.

DOOGIE HOWSER, M.D. (Neil Patrick Harris) is a sixteen-year-old resident doctor at Eastman Medical Center who is still living at home with his doctor father David and mother Katherine. He gets support from them as well as from hospital chief-of-staff Dr. Benjamin Canfield and fellow resident Jack McGuire.

1984 September 16 MIAMI VICE (NBC). Det. Sonny Crockett (Don Johnson), Det. Ricardo Tubbs (Philip Michael Thomas), Lt. Martin Castillo (Edward James Olmos), Det. Gina Calabrese (Saundra Santiago), Det. Trudy Joplin (Olivia Brown). Don Johnson's career soared during the run of this stylish, sexy show. Lt. Castillo was the senior officer to whom Crockett and Tubbs reported. **September 30 MURDER, SHE WROTE** (CBS). Jessica Fletcher (Angela Lansbury), Sheriff Amos Tupper (Tom Bosley), Grady Fletcher (Michael Horton), Dr. Seth Hazlitt (William Windom). Crime novelist Jessica Fletcher each week solved a mystery almost always set in the small Maine town of Cabot Cove, although she later moved to New York City and solved mysteries from there. Plots were intricate and adult

Centered around a family member with Down's syndrome, LIFE GOES ON was a prime-time drama. The Thatcher family included Drew Thatcher (Bill Smitrovich), his wife Libby (Patti LuPone), Corky (Christopher Burke) their eighteen-year-old son with Down's syndrome, Paige (Monique Lanier) the older daughter, and Becca (Kellie Martin) as the younger daughter, who is in the same grade in school as Corky.

and appealed to mystery book readers. **1985 September 14 THE GOLDEN GIRLS** (NBC). First sitcom with all characters over 50, all female, and all interested in romance. Set in Miami. Four roommates: divorced teacher Dorothy Zbornak (Bea Arthur), grief counselor Rose Nylund (Betty White), home owner and museum employee Blanche Devereaux (Rue McClanahan), Dorothy's mother Sophia Petrillo (Estelle Getty). **September 29 MacGYVER** (ABC). Working at the Phoenix Foundation, ex-Special Forces Agent MacGyver (Richard Dean Anderson) fights (usually without weapons) for right on international assignments from Director of Field Operations Peter Thornton (Dana Elcar).

THE SIMPSONS began as short sketches on *The Tracey Ullman Show* and became a humorous prime-time animated series for adults that touches on serious subjects of contemporary life.

The final two-hour broadcast of DALLAS, May 3, 1991, was one of TV's most-watched episodes. The show starred Larry Hagman as the notorious Texas oilman J.R. Ewing.

Mystery writer Jessica Fletcher (Angela Lansbury) solved crime cases each week on MURDER, SHE WROTE.

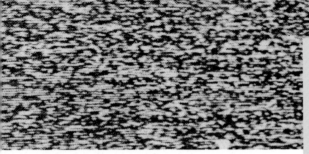

1986 **September 8 THE OPRAH WINFREY SHOW** (syndicated). Daytime talk show hosted by Oprah Winfrey. One of the most successful TV shows ever, with guests, a book segment (that creates overnight bestsellers).

September 15 L.A. LAW (NBC). Created by *Hill St. Blues'* Steven Bochco and *Cagney & Lacey's* Terry Louise Fisher, the legal office/courtroom drama dealt with newsworthy legal/social issues. Law firm staff of McKensie, Brackman, Chaney and Kusak included: Senior partner Leland McKenzie (Richard Dysart); Douglas Brackman, Jr. (Alan Rachins); Michael Kusak (Harry Hamlin); Asst. D.A. Grace Van Owen (Susan Dey); lawyer Ann Kelsey (Jill Eikenberry); accountant Stuart Markowitz (Michael Tucker), who later marries Kelsey after he demonstrates the unexplained sexual maneuver "Venus Butterfly"; divorce lawyer who chases women Arnie Becker (Corbin Bersen); lawyer Victor Sifuentes (Jimmy Smits); Becker's hardworking secretary Roxanne Melman (Susan Ruttan); lawyer and single parent Abby Perkins (Michele Greene). Some stories carried over from week to week (especially the intimate lives of the main characters).

TWIN PEAKS. A very unusual twisting, somewhat spooky drama created by David Lynch and Mark Frost. "Who killed Laura Palmer?" was the case that brought agent Dale Cooper (Kyle MacLachlan) to the town of Twin Peaks. He is here with Harry S. Truman (Michael Ontkean), mayor of the town. Coffee and doughnuts were ever present.

1987 April 5 MARRIED...WITH CHILDREN (FOX). The Bundy family: father Al (Ed O'Neill), mother Peg (Katey Sagal), Kelly (Christina Applegate), Bud (David Faustino), live in a suburb of Chicago. Not your typical family values show. The almost cartoon-like Bundys fought, put each other down, had low expectations, and thought about sex all the time. A controversial and very successful comedy. **September 22 FULL HOUSE** (ABC). Three men and three cute kids formed a household in San Francisco that grew each season as other characters were added. The very popular Olsen twins (Mary Kate and Ashley Fuller) jointly played the youngest child. Danny Tanner (Bob Saget), Jesse Cochran (John Stamos), Danny's uncle, Joey Gladstsone (David Coulier) are all in some aspect of show business. **September 29 THIRTY-SOMETHING** (ABC). In the 1980s (before Gen-X became hot), yuppies in their 30s were the audience to go after. Set in Philadelphia, two couples Michael (Ken Olin) and Hope Steadman (Mel Harris) and Elliot (Timothy Busfield) and Nancy Weston (Patricia Wettig), their children, and various single friends—Ellyn (Polly Draper) and Prof. Gary Shepherd (Peter Horton)—anguished over the meaning of their very upper-middle-class lives. Michael and Elliot opened their own advertising agency, which had ups and downs, as did their marriages and relationships. This show resonated with viewers of the same age. **October STAR TREK: THE NEXT GENERATION** (syndicated). Rather formal Capt. Jean-Luc Picard (Patrick Stewart); second-in-command Cmdr. William Riker (Jonathan Frakes); blind Lt. Geordi La Forge (LeVar Burton) who could "see" with a special visor; Klingon officer Lt. Worf (Michael Dorn); the *Enterprise*'s medical doctor Beverly Crusher (Gates McFadden); Counselor Deanna Troi (Marina Sirtis), who could feel and sense everyone's emotions; android with a "positronic brain", Lt. Cmdr. Data (Brent Spiner); Dr. Crusher's son Wesley Crusher (Wil Wheaton) an aspiring Star Fleet officer. The 24th century (the earlier Star Trek was set in the 23rd), a new *Enterprise*, new sleek uniforms, new crew—still defenders of justice in the Federation.

A quiz show with a twist. JEOPARDY! gives contestants the answers and they have to give their responses in form of a question ("What is...?"). Material on this show is fairly difficult and there are no histrionics from the three contestants. They hold buzzers to signal when they know an answer and get down to business by choosing a category from the lit board (each answer has a dollar amount attached and a wrong response has that amount deducted). After the Final Jeopardy round, prizes are awarded for the most money accumulated.

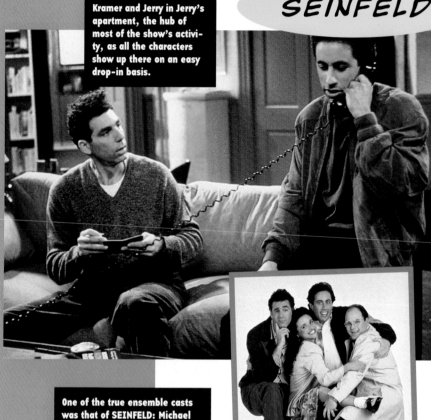

SEINFELD

Kramer and Jerry in Jerry's apartment, the hub of most of the show's activity, as all the characters show up there on an easy drop-in basis.

One of the true ensemble casts was that of SEINFELD: Michael Richards as Cosmo Kramer, Julia Louis-Dreyfus as Elaine Benes, Jerry Seinfeld as himself, and Jason Alexander as George Costanza. The show about "nothing," one of the highest rated ever, brought New York angst and superficiality to a new comic and popular level.

1988 **January 31 THE WONDER YEARS**
(ABC). Theme song "With a Little Help from My Friends" sung by Joe Cocker. Narrated by an adult Kevin Arnold (Daniel Stern, voice only), the story focused on 12-year-old Kevin (Fred Savage) growing up in the 1960s in the suburbs. Kevin, older brother Wayne (Jason Hervey), sister Karen (Olivia d'Abo), lived with mother Norma (Alley Mills) and father Jack (Dan Lauria). Plots centered on Kevin's life in school, dating, dealing with parents, and trying to fit in. **October 18 ROSEANNE** (ABC). One of the most popular of the blue-collar family sitcoms. The Conner family: Roseanne (Roseanne), Dan (John Goodman), the kids Becky (Lecy Goranson, then Sarah Chalke), Darlene (Sara Gilbert), D.J. (Michael Fishman), Roseanne's sister Jackie (Laurie Metcalf). Realistically hefty parents who are sometimes out of work, foul-mouthed kids, never enough money, an afghan thrown over the couch back—all realistic touches for this basically good-humored, good-natured family who did love each other despite the ups and downs. Enormously popular. **November 14 MURPHY BROWN** (CBS). Veteran TV reporter Murphy Brown (Candice Bergen), 25-year TV anchorman Jim Dial (Charles Kimbrough), reporter Frank Fontana (Joe Regalbuto), perky young reporter Corky Sherwood (Faith Ford), executive producer Miles Silverberg (Grant Shaud), bartender Phil (Pat Corley). Clever articulate funny dialogue. TV newscasters for "FYI" based in Washington, D.C. Jockeying for position on air and off. Real-life celebrities appeared on the show.

George, in one of his rare jobs lasting more than a few weeks, works as Assistant to the Traveling Secretary of the New York Yankees. Here he is seen discussing strategy with Jerry.

1989 September 12 LIFE GOES ON (ABC). Restaurant owner Drew Thatcher (Bill Smitrovich), his wife former singer Libby (Patti LuPone), daughter Becca (Kellie Martin), Drew's daughter Paige (Monique Lanier) all cope with life with Corky (Christopher Burke), a Down's syndrome son. Corky is finally going to high school at age 18 and finds himself in the same class with younger sister Becca. A warm and funny series. **September 19 DOOGIE HOWSER, M.D.** (ABC). Sixteen-year-old genius Doogie Howser (Neil Patrick Harris) is a second-year medical resident at Eastman Medical Center in L.A. His incongruous age and his medical responsibilities are at the core of the show. **September 22 FAMILY MATTERS** (ABC). Spin-off of *Perfect Strangers*, focuses on the nerdy Steve Urkel (Jaleel White), whose character didn't show up until episode nine, when he immediately became popular.

GERALDO RIVERA, as do other top-rated talk show hosts, leads a single-topic audience participation show. He has been controversial for choosing sensational topics throughout his career and is remembered for a show in which a fight broke out and Geraldo had his nose broken on the air.

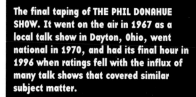

The final taping of THE PHIL DONAHUE SHOW. It went on the air in 1967 as a local talk show in Dayton, Ohio, went national in 1970, and had its final hour in 1996 when ratings fell with the influx of many talk shows that covered similar subject matter.

THE OPRAH WINFREY SHOW outper-
formed every other talk show. Winfrey
became one of the wealthiest television
personalities when she formed her own
production company for this and other
television projects. Her topics tend to be
more serious than those on other talk
shows and her recent move into book
club segments has helped create instant
best-sellers.

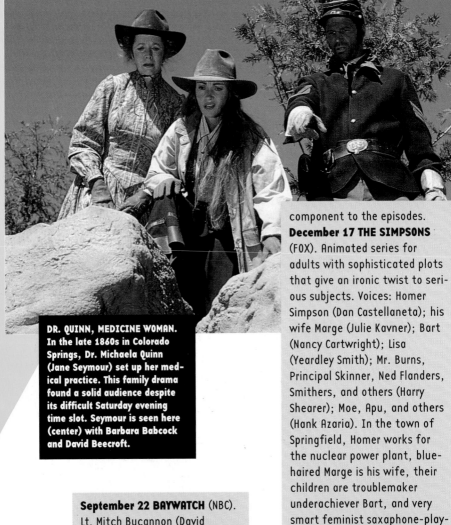

DR. QUINN, MEDICINE WOMAN. In the late 1860s in Colorado Springs, Dr. Michaela Quinn (Jane Seymour) set up her medical practice. This family drama found a solid audience despite its difficult Saturday evening time slot. Seymour is seen here (center) with Barbara Babcock and David Beecroft.

September 22 BAYWATCH (NBC). Lt. Mitch Bucannon (David Hasselhoff) oversees the Malibu Beach lifeguards. This globally popular hour-long drama has scantily clad lifeguards reacting to rescue efforts in the water and out. Often there is a crime component to the episodes.

December 17 THE SIMPSONS (FOX). Animated series for adults with sophisticated plots that give an ironic twist to serious subjects. Voices: Homer Simpson (Dan Castellaneta); his wife Marge (Julie Kavner); Bart (Nancy Cartwright); Lisa (Yeardley Smith); Mr. Burns, Principal Skinner, Ned Flanders, Smithers, and others (Harry Shearer); Moe, Apu, and others (Hank Azaria). In the town of Springfield, Homer works for the nuclear power plant, blue-haired Marge is his wife, their children are troublemaker underachiever Bart, and very smart feminist saxophone-playing Lisa, baby Maggie, who never talks and always has a pacifier. Celebrity guest voices (and characters) have included Ringo Starr, Jackie Mason, and Tony Bennett.

FRIENDS. A highly popular prime-time sitcom. Living in New York is a group of friends in their 20s, who often meet at the Central Perk Cafe, where one of them works as a waitress. The drama centers around jobs, dating, parenthood, divorce, and just getting along in New York.

1990 April 8 TWIN PEAKS (ABC). Spooky drama. Agent Dale Cooper (Kyle MacLachlan) came to the northwestern town of Twin Peaks, which was populated by some very strange characters. He came to solve a murder case that created widespread initial viewer interest, but it lasted only a year after the plot twists changed the avid audience's need to know "who was that dancing dwarf?" and "what happened then?" to "who cares." **May 31 SEINFELD** (NBC). The top-rated comedy show. Jerry Seinfeld (Jerry Seinfeld), Elaine Benes (Julia Louis-Dreyfus), George Costanza (Jason Alexander), Cosmo Kramer (Michael Richards). Jerry, a stand-up comic, lives in a NY apartment across the hall from the almost-always-unemployed Kramer, who continually has schemes afloat and seems to always have a means of support.

TOUCHED BY AN ANGEL, featuring three angels— Andrew, a kind "angel of death" (John Dye), Monica (Roma Downey), and Tess, Monica's "supervisor" (Della Reese)—who are sent to Earth to help solve worldly problems. This non-denominational but openly religious show has a large following.

George is Jerry's closest friend, and he too has trouble keeping a job, although his ability to embellish on nonexistent credentials ("I'm a marine biologist") lands him new possibilities. Elaine is Jerry's ex-girlfriend and current close friend. Each episode has simple plots interweaving with long-term plot elements. Superficial relationships (all are in their 30s and unmarried) and dating opportunities in New York City are key. George's parents are hilariously played deadpan by Estelle Harris and Jerry Stiller. The final episode aired May 14, 1998, and was one of the most watched in TV history. **June 16 JEOPARDY!** (ABC). Hosted by Art Fleming for the first season (1964) and then Alex Trebek. A quiz show in which answers are revealed and the contestants must give the question. Material is usually fairly difficult. **July 12 NORTHERN EXPOSURE** (CBS). In order to fulfill a medical school commitment, young New York City doctor Joel Fleischman (Rob Morrow) lands in a tiny Alaskan village called Cicely and copes with culture shock. Key characters are Maggie O'Connell (Janine Turner); rich ex-astronaut Maurice Minnifield (Barry Corbin); Native American Ed Chigliak (Darren E. Burrows); bar owner and mayor

Starring Claire Danes as the angst-ridden fifteen-year-old Angela Chase, MY SO-CALLED LIFE was on-air for only one season. It was intelligent drama from the point of view of tenth-grader Angela.

Holling Vincoeur (John Collum); Shelly Tombo (Cynthia Geary), waitress and eventually wife of Holling; Marilyn Whirlwind (Elaine Miles), Joel's single-minded Native American assistant; Ruth-Anne Miller (Peg Phillips), owner of the general store; Chris Stevens (John Corbett), the town's DJ. The interweaving of cultures gave this unusual show its interest.

MELROSE PLACE year 4. A spin-off of *Beverly Hills 90210*, this show proved equally popular. Here are Andrew Shue as Billy Campbell and Kristen Davis as Brooke Armstrong, his wife.

MAD ABOUT YOU. Young married New Yorkers, documentary filmmaker Paul Buchman (Paul Reiser) and PR exec Jamie (Helen Hunt), live in an apartment with baby Mabel and their dog Murray. Their domestic life is the focus of this very popular sitcom.

September 10 THE FRESH PRINCE OF BEL-AIR (NBC). Will Smith (played by Will Smith, AKA rap musician Fresh Prince) moves from Philadelphia to live with well-to-do family relatives in Bel Air, California: lawyer uncle Philip Banks (James Avery); aunt Vivian Banks (Janet Hubert); cousins Carlton (Alfonso Ribeiro), Hilary (Karyn Parsons), and Ashley (Tatyana M. Ali). They have a butler called Geoffrey Butler (Joseph Marcell). The story revolves around the family and Will and Carlton's time as students in college and their relationships. **1991 September 17 HOME IMPROVEMENT** (ABC). Tim Taylor (comedian Tim Allen) who

LOVING COUPLES

hosts a TV show called "Tool Time" with Al Borland (Richard Karn), wife Jill Taylor (Patricia Richardson), sons Brad (Zachary Ty Bryan), Randy (Jonathan Taylor Thomas), Mark (Tarna Smith). Shows center on the running of the household and Tim's knack for "fixing" things. **1992 September 23 MAD ABOUT YOU** (NBC). In contemporary New York City, married couple Paul Buchman (Paul Reiser) and wife Jamie (Helen Hunt) lived for years with just their dog Murray. In the 1997 season they give birth to Mabel, giving an added plot element for the humor.

BEVERLY HILLS 90210 year 6.
This show has a wide teenaged audience, since much of the plot lines involve teenagers. Here are Jennie Garth as Kelly Taylor with Jason Wiles, who plays Colin.

CYBILL. In this sitcom, Cybill Sheridan (Cybill Shepherd) and best friend Maryann Thorpe (Christine Baranski) deal with Cybill's daughters, her ex-husbands, and Maryann's ex, "Dr. Dick," as well as Cybill's ongoing attempts to continue her career as an actress.

1993 January 1 DR. QUINN, MEDICINE WOMAN (CBS). Set in the late 1860s in Colorado Springs. Dr. Michaela ("Dr. Mike") Quinn (Jane Seymour) sets up medical practice and also adopts three children after one of her patients dies. She first rents a house from and then marries Byron Sully (Joe Lando) a woodsman. They also have their own child. **April 22 WALKER, TEXAS RANGER** (CBS) stars the very popular actor Chuck Norris as Cordell Walker, a contemporary Texas ranger who solves crimes the old fashioned way—with his fists. He is joined by the more cerebral Jimmy Trevette (Clarence Gilyard) in crime busting.

Fran Drescher, who plays THE NANNY, works for wealthy New York widower Maxwell Sheffield. Her exaggerated, nasal, Long Island accent, her over-the-top fashion sense, and her sense of humor are central features of the show. She is seen here with Renee Taylor, who plays her even more outrageous mother.

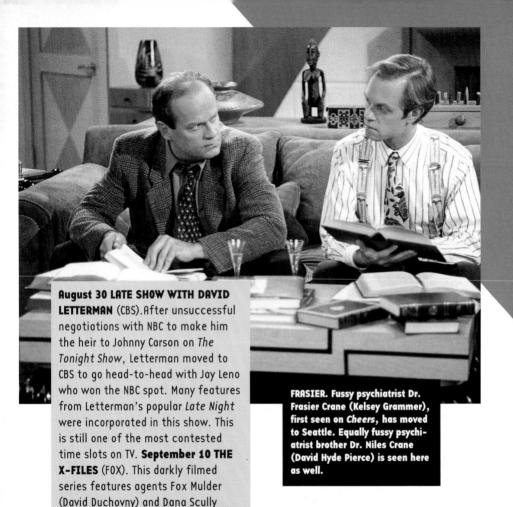

August 30 LATE SHOW WITH DAVID LETTERMAN (CBS). After unsuccessful negotiations with NBC to make him the heir to Johnny Carson on *The Tonight Show*, Letterman moved to CBS to go head-to-head with Jay Leno who won the NBC spot. Many features from Letterman's popular *Late Night* were incorporated in this show. This is still one of the most contested time slots on TV. **September 10 THE X-FILES** (FOX). This darkly filmed series features agents Fox Mulder (David Duchovny) and Dana Scully (Gillian Anderson) who are investigating various unsolved cases in the X-Files. Much of the work involves alien encounters and other unexplained phenomena, and many cases remain unsolved. The look of the program and its content have made it into an instant cult classic. **September 16 FRASIER** (NBC). A comedy spin-off of

FRASIER. Fussy psychiatrist Dr. Frasier Crane (Kelsey Grammer), first seen on *Cheers*, has moved to Seattle. Equally fussy psychiatrist brother Dr. Niles Crane (David Hyde Pierce) is seen here as well.

Veteran reporter **MURPHY BROWN** (Candice Bergen) works at "FYI," a television news magazine program based in Washington, D.C. She is seen here with Paul Rubens who plays a nephew of the station owner and Murphy's super-efficient sometime secretary. This intelligent sitcom got a lot of real-world response including from then-Vice President Dan Quayle, who thought that Murphy's on-air single motherhood did not uphold appropriate family values.

Cheers. Psychiatrist Frasier Crane (Kelsey Grammer) moves to Seattle after his divorce from Lilith (Bebe Neuwirth) and becomes the host of a radio advice show. Roz Doyle (Peri Gilpin) is his feisty producer. His police detective father Martin (John Mahoney) retires after being shot and moves in with him. Daphne Moon (Jane Leeves) is Martin's offbeat live-in home care worker, who claims to have psychic powers. Brother Dr. Niles Crane (David Hyde Pierce), also a psychiatrist, lives in Seattle. Comedy centers on the neurotic actions of Frasier and Niles.

NASH BRIDGES (Don Johnson) and partner Joe Dominguez (Cheech Marin) are the duo to watch in this sexy San Francisco cop show. They are seen here with some cast members of *Miami Vice*.

November 3 THE NANNY (CBS). Fran Fine (Fran Drescher) works as a nanny for a wealthy New York widower, Maxwell Sheffield (Charles Shaughnessy), with three children. Fran's love for Sheffield and her notable Long Island nasal speech trigger many of the laughs on this very popular sitcom. **1994 March 29 ELLEN (THESE FRIENDS OF MINE)** (ABC). Bookstore owner Ellen Morgan (Ellen DeGeneres) and various friends deal with every-day life on this sitcom. The 1997 season focused on the "coming out" of lesbian Ellen. The episode in which Ellen admits to Oprah Winfrey (who played Ellen's therapist) and to romantic inter-est Laura Dern that she is gay was one of the most watched of that season.

THE X-FILES. This dark series of mini-movies has special agents Fox Mulder (David Duchovny) and Dana Scully (Gillian Anderson) investigate various unsolved cases in the X-Files. Mulder is haunted by what he believes was an alien abduction of his sister; Scully is more scientific and skeptical. Much of their work involves alien encounters and other unexplained phenomena.

The cast of ER, the highest rated of the new crop of medical dramas. The plot lines, the heightened pace in the Emergency Room of a big-city hospital, and the close-up camera work, create a riveting weekly drama. Opposite is a typical filled-with-drama scene in the operating room.

E R

September 21 TOUCHED BY AN ANGEL (CBS). Tess (Della Reese) and Monica (Roma Downey) are angels who help people solve some of their worldly problems. When death cannot be avoided, a male angel, Andrew (John Dye), arrives to ease the passage. An openly inspirational, religious bent to this drama series. **September 22 FRIENDS** (NBC). Revolving around six friends in their 20s living in New York City who mostly hang out at a coffee bar where Rachel Green (Jennifer Aniston) waitresses. Her roommate Monica Geller (Courtney Cox), Phoebe Buffay (Lisa Kudrow), Joey Tribbiani (Matt LeBlanc), his roommate Chandler Bing (Matthew Perry), Monica's brother Ross Geller (David Schwimmer) are the key characters.

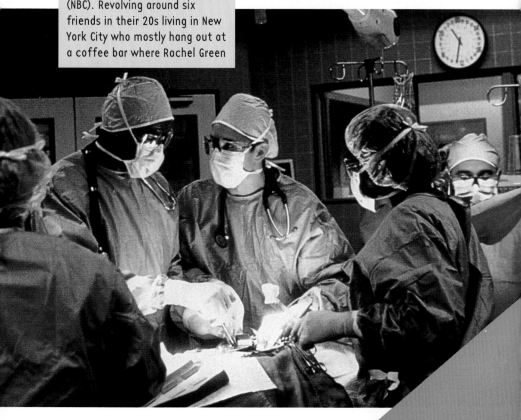

BROOKLYN SOUTH: Francis X. Donovan (Jon Tenney) and Officer Ann-Marie Kersey (Yancy Butler).

BROOKLYN SOUTH: This police drama premiered with a show in which the streets of Brooklyn becomes a war zone when a shooting spree occurs. Both civilians and police are killed. The gunman is apprehended, but then dies while in police custody, prompting an investigation of police conduct.

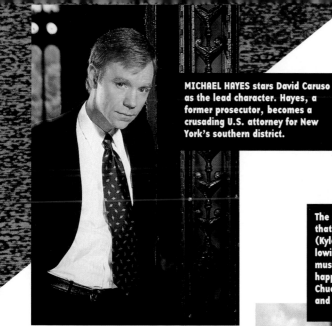

MICHAEL HAYES stars David Caruso as the lead character. Hayes, a former prosecutor, becomes a crusading U.S. attorney for New York's southern district.

The premise of **EARLY EDITION** is that each morning Gary Hobson (Kyle Chandler) receives the following day's newspaper and he must prevent bad news from happening. Other key cast are Chuck Fishman (Fisher Stevens) and Robin (Ellen Mills).

1995 January 2 CYBILL (CBS). In this comedy, Cybill Sheridan (Cybill Shepherd) and best friend Maryann Thorpe (Christine Baranski) deal with Cybill's two ex-husbands and her daughters Rachel (Dedee Pfeiffer) and Zoey (Alicia Witt) as Cybill continually tries to get work as an actress and usually ends up in odd situations. **January 11 THE WAYANS BROS.** (WB). Marlon (Marlon Wayans) and Shawn (Shawn Wayans), father Pop (John Witherspoon), Lisa (Lela Rochon) Shawn's girlfriend, The brothers are seeking their fortune in a series of intricate plans.

September 13 THE DREW CAREY SHOW (ABC). Set in Cleveland, Ohio. Drew Carey (comedian Drew Carey) is the assistant director of personnel at a department store; his friends are Oswald (Diedrich Bader) a DJ, Lewis (Ryan Stiles) a janitor, and Kate (Christa Miller). **1996 January 9 THIRD ROCK FROM THE SUN** (NBC) features a "family" of aliens posing as barely credible but quirky Earthlings. The show stars John Lithgow (as Dick Solomon) who works with Jane Curtin (as Mary Albright) and has a crush on her. **March 29 NASH BRIDGES** (CBS). A high-action cop drama set in San Francisco and starring Don Johnson as Bridges and

DIAGNOSIS MURDER. Dick Van Dyke (center front) is Dr. Mark Sloan, an amateur crime solver who works at Community General Hospital.

Cheech Marin as his partner, the wisecracking Joe Dominguez. Nash is a great detective, but is less able to manage his personal life involving two ex-wives and a teenaged daughter. Sexy and fast paced. **September 13 EVERYBODY LOVES RAYMOND** (CBS). Ray Barone (Ray Romano) is married and is the father of a young daughter and younger twin sons. His extended family lives nearby, and this comedy centers around chaotic family life. **September 17 SPIN CITY** (ABC) starring Michael J. Fox as Deputy Mayor of New York Michael Flaherty in charge of PR for the mayor (played by Barry Bostwick). Unfolding political crises and the mayor's often embarassing responses to them are the focus of this sitcom. **September 18 MEN BEHAVING BADLY** (NBC) featured two obnoxious guy roommates Jamie (Rob Schneider) and Kevin (Ron Eldard), who offended almost everybody. Sarah (Justine Bateman) was Kevin's long-suffering girlfriend. **September 19 SUDDENLY SUSAN** (NBC). A show starring Brooke Shields as a San Francisco magazine writer. The sitcom focuses on the thirtyish Susan's work and personal life. **1997** 2.8 billion TV sets worldwide. 98 percent of U.S. households have a color TV.

THE GREGORY HINES SHOW.
Gregory Hines, tap dancer extraordinaire, does not dance in this new show. Here he plays Ben Stevenson, father to Matthew "Matty" (Brandon Hammond).

January 12 KING OF THE HILL
(FOX), an animated prime-time family sitcom featuring a blue-collar family from Texas. The father works at Strickland Propane company, his wife Peggy is a substitute Spanish teacher, niece Luanne is studying to be a beautician, and son

Young lawyer **ALLY McBEAL (Calista Flockhart)** joins a small firm and finds that her ex-boyfriend (now married) also works there. Their emotional interactions and Ally's fantasy life, which is either heard in her voice-over narration or shown on screen, comprise some of the main plot lines for this stylish drama.

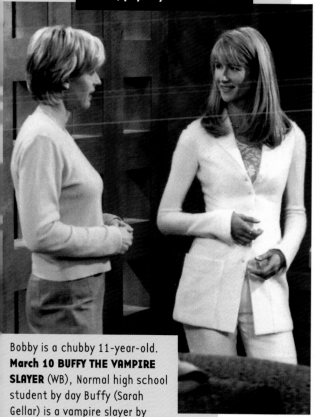

This April 30, 1997, episode of ELLEN was one of the most anticipated and most watched of the season. It is the one in which bookstore owner Ellen (Ellen DeGeneres) comes out as a lesbian. She is here with her love interest, played by Laura Dern.

Bobby is a chubby 11-year-old. **March 10 BUFFY THE VAMPIRE SLAYER** (WB), Normal high school student by day Buffy (Sarah Gellar) is a vampire slayer by night. Two other vampire slayers and various friends, along with mentor Anthony Head, help Buffy with the undead. **September 8 ALLY McBEAL** (FOX). Young lawyer Ally McBeal (Calista Flockhart) joins a small firm and finds that her ex-boyfriend Billy Thomas (Gil Bellows) also works there. He is now married to Georgia (*Melrose Place*'s Courtney Thorne-Smith), but Ally stills confides in him with personal problems. One of the innovative features of the script is that Ally's fantasy life is either learned through a voice-over narrative or in very innovative fantasy sequences such as Ally dancing with an Internet-created tiny "virtual" baby. **September 15 GEORGE AND LEO** (CBS). Two television veterans, Bob Newhart (who plays George) and Judd Hirsch (Leo) team up for this sitcom. George's son is about to marry Leo's daughter; Leo is an ex-con who is supposed to be in hiding from the mob, but is instead very much involved with the soon-to-be-joined families. **September 25 VERONICA'S CLOSET** (NBC) stars *Cheers* success Kirstie Alley as Ronnie, the head of a lingerie business called Veronica's Closet. Ronnie's dwindling romantic life is the center of this sitcom. **1998 March 23 THE "OSCARS"** (ABC). Watched by 86 million viewers in the U.S., the Academy Awards ran long (almost 4 hours) and was seen for fashion as much as for the suspense of naming the winners.

Acknowledgments

We would like to acknowledge the following individuals who helped us during the book-making process:

First we would like to thank Ann Limongello (ABC, Inc.), Bruce Pomerantz (CBS, Inc.), and Ray Whelan, Jr. (Globe Photos) for supplying the images for this volume.

Tim Jeffs provided technical help and support. Shari Berman assisted with fact checking; Teri Leggio with editing. Both are highly knowledgable about TV and are fanatic fans of the medium. For the cover: Kosta Potamianos created the illustration; Charles Lee helped with last-minute electronic pre-press work. Leslie LaRue helped with the photograph credits.

We thank our families for putting up with our long obsessive hours in front of the computer. We also would like to thank Drs. Bill Gilson, Peter Geller, and Thomas Garrett for helping us survive during this period.

At Harry N. Abrams, Inc., we thank President Paul Gottlieb for his enthusiastic support of this project. Heartfelt thanks as well to Director of Special Projects Robert Morton and his associate Nola Butler for their attention to details and for keeping us on deadline.

About this book

TV MANIA was conceived by Pavese & Henry Books. Edith Pavese wrote the captions and timeline; Pavese and Henry jointly selected the images; Judith Henry designed the book.

The book was designed and the layout was prepared on the Macintosh G3 in QuarkXPress 4.0. The type for the captions and timeline in this book is Base Twelve Sans, which is an Emigre typeface designed by Zuzana Licko in 1995. The font was designed first as a multimedia screen font and then reworked for print media.

PHOTOGRAPH CREDITS

The authors wish to thank the organizations listed below for supplying the photographs for this project. Images are listed in the order in which they appear in the book. Photographers' names, when available, appear in parentheses after the © notice.

Howdy Doody ©NBC/Globe Photos, Inc.; *The Ed Sullivan Show (Toast of the Town)* CBS Photo Archive; *The Milton Berle Show (Texaco Star Theater)* ©NBC/Globe Photos, Inc.; *The Goldbergs* CBS Photo Archive; *Hopalong Cassidy* ©NBC/Globe Photos, Inc.; *Beat the Clock* CBS Photo Archive; *Your Show of Shows* ©NBC/Globe Photos, Inc.; *Your Hit Parade* ©NBC/Globe Photos, Inc.; *Mama* CBS Photo Archive; *Take a Good Look* ©1997 ABC, Inc.; *I Love Lucy* CBS Photo Archive; *Kukla, Fran and Ollie* ©1997 ABC, Inc.; *Strike It Rich* CBS Photo Archive; *Alfred Hitchcock Presents* CBS Photo Archive; *The Jack Benny Show* CBS Photo Archive; *Our Miss Brooks* CBS Photo Archive; *Ozzie and Harriet* ©1997 ABC, Inc.; *Arthur Godfrey's Talent Scouts* CBS Photo Archive; *The Red Buttons Show* CBS Photo Archive; *This Is Your Life* ©NBC/Globe Photos, Inc.; *Dragnet* ©NBC/Globe Photos, Inc.; *Life With Father* CBS Photo Archive; *Lassie* CBS Photo Archive; *What's My Line* CBS Photo Archive; *Father Knows Best* ©1997 ABC, Inc.; *The Honeymooners* CBS Photo Archive; *The Mickey Mouse Club* ©1997 ABC, Inc.; *Captain Kangaroo* CBS Photo Archive; *Lawrence Welk* ©1997 ABC, Inc.; *Gunsmoke* CBS Photo Archive; *Cheyenne* ©1997 ABC, Inc.; *The Life and Legend of Wyatt Earp* ©1997 ABC, Inc.; *You'll Never Get Rich (The Phil Silvers Show)* CBS Photo Archive; *To Tell The Truth* CBS Photo Archive; *Leave It To Beaver* CBS Photo Archive; *Have Gun, Will Travel* CBS Photo Archive; *The Price Is Right* ©NBC/Globe Photos, Inc.; *American Bandstand* ©1997 ABC, Inc.; *The Many Loves of Dobie Gillis* CBS Photo Archive; *As the World Turns* CBS Photo Archive; *Dick Clark* ©NBC/Globe Photos, Inc.; *The Millionaire* CBS Photo Archive; *Wagon Train* NBC/Globe Photos, Inc.; *Maverick* ©1997 ABC, Inc.; *Bonanza* NBC/Globe Photos, Inc.; *Zorro* ©1997 ABC, Inc.; *Rawhide* CBS Photo Archives; *Wanted Dead or Alive* CBS Photo Archive; *The Flintstones* ©1997 ABC, Inc.; *Queen for a Day* ©1997 ABC, Inc.; *77 Sunset Strip* ©1997 ABC, Inc.; *Perry Mason* CBS Photo Archive; *My Three Sons* ©1997 ABC, Inc.; *Route 66* CBS Photo Archive; *The Untouchables* ©1997 ABC, Inc.; *Dr. Kildare* © NBC/Globe Photos, Inc.; *I've Got A Secret* CBS Photo Archive; *The Dick Van Dyke Show* CBS Photo Archive; *Hazel* ©NBC/Globe Photos, Inc.; *The Twilight Zone* CBS Photo Archive; *The Guiding Light* CBS Photo Archive; *Ben Casey* ©1997 ABC, Inc.; *As the World Turns* CBS Photo Archive; *The Tonight Show* ©NBC/Globe Photos, Inc.; *The Ed Sullivan Show* CBS Photo Archive; *Star Trek* © NBC/Globe Photos, Inc.; *The Fugitive* ©1997 ABC, Inc; *The Jetsons* ©1997 ABC, Inc.; *Gilligan's Island* CBS Photo Archive; *The Tennessee Ernie Ford Hour* ©NBC/Globe Photos, Inc.; *Bewitched* ©1997 ABC, Inc.; *Candid Camera* CBS Photo Archive; *The Munsters* CBS Photo Archive; *Petticoat Junction* CBS Photo Archive; *I Dream of Jeannie* ©NBC/Globe Photos, Inc.; *Peyton Place* ©1997 ABC, Inc.; *The Steve Allen Show* CBS Photo Archive; *The Beverly Hillbillies* CBS Photo Archive; *That Girl* ©1997 ABC, Inc.; *Mission Impossible* CBS Photo Archive; *Dark Shadows* ©1997 ABC, Inc.; *Let's Make a Deal* ©NBC/Globe Photos, Inc.; *The Carol Burnett Show* CBS Photo Archive; *The Smothers Brothers* CBS Photo Archive; *The Flying Nun* ©1997 ABC, Inc.; *Rowan & Martin's Laugh-In* ©NBC/Globe Photos, Inc.; *60 Minutes* CBS Photo Archive; *Hollywood Squares* ©NBC/Globe Photos, Inc.; *Hee Haw* CBS Photo Archive; *The Brady Bunch* ©1997 ABC, Inc.; *The Partridge Family* ©1997 ABC, Inc.; *Hawaii Five-0* CBS Photo Archive; *Marcus Welby, M.D.* ©1997 ABC, Inc.; *The Mary Tyler Moore Show* CBS Photo Archive; *All in the Family* CBS Photo Archive; *Columbo* ©NBC/Globe Photos, Inc.; *M*A*S*H* CBS Photo Archive; *The Bob Newhart Show* CBS Photo

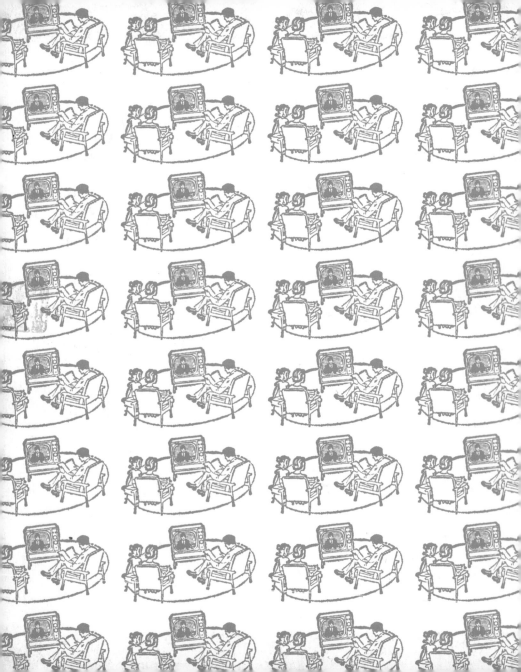